D0923449

CHRISTIAN POETRY

IS VOLUME

118

OF THE

Twentieth Century Encyclopedia of Catholicism

UNDER SECTION

XI

CATHOLICISM AND LITERATURE

IT IS ALSO THE

130TH

VOLUME IN ORDER OF PUBLICATION

Edited by HENRI DANIEL-ROPS of the Académie Française

CHRISTIAN POETRY

By ELIZABETH JENNINGS

HAWTHORN BOOKS · PUBLISHERS · *New York*

First Edition, April, 1965

NIHIL OBSTAT

Joannes M. T. Barton, S.T.D., L.S.S.

Censor Deputatus

IMPRIMATUR

Patritius Casey

Vicarius Generalis

Westmonasterii, die XIX FEBRUARII MCMLXV

The Nihil obstat and Imprimatur are a declaration that a book or pamphlet is considered to be free from doctrinal or moral error. It is not implied that those who have granted the Nihil obstat and Imprimatur agree with the contents, opinions, or statements expressed.

CONTENTS

CHAPTER I

INTRODUCTION TO CHRISTIAN POETRY

In a study as brief as this, it is not possible to cover the whole field of Christian poetry, to examine its manifestations in every country and every century. Such an attempt would be not only futile, but fruitless. At the best, it would produce a mere catalogue of names and dates, and, at the worst, an essay so densely packed with mere facts and opinions that, after examining it, the reader would be none the wiser.

I propose, therefore, to do two things: firstly, to make this a *personal* book, a view of Christian poetry which proceeds from my own predilections and preferences, and, secondly, to take a handful of Christian poets and poems (mostly English) of various periods and to try to find in them what belongs specifically to Christianity: thus, I shall be working from the particular to the general. Such an approach will, I hope, at least be clear, even if it is very restricted. I do not propose to look in detail at many foreign Christian poets; my knowledge of languages other than English is very limited and one needs to know a language deeply and thoroughly before one can hope to say anything useful about a particular literature.

Many difficulties are involved in setting about writing a book which has the nature of this one. The author is beset with problems of taste and fashion, dogma and belief,

style and form, tradition and the *avant-garde*, as well as
with the questions which force any critic who is attempting
to link a personal commentary with historical facts. For,
in many ways, Christian poetry is no different from any
other kind of verse; if it is good and lasting, this is not
because it is Christian poetry but because it is fine poetry.
Too many earnest Catholics have been brought up to judge
the matter rather than the manner of a so-called Christian
poem; hence the appalling standard of most of our hymns
and prayers in the vernacular. At a time like this, when
the liturgical movement is very lively within the Church,
although outside it there appears to exist a state of almost
complete lassitude, at least among the young, towards
Christianity (Catholicism, of course, has known worse
periods before, though this is certainly no excuse for us
to rest smugly in our sense of history, or to expect God
and the Pope to do everything for us)—if all this is so, then
we can ill afford to produce and promulgate a poetry that
is shoddy, dishonest and lacking in life and enthusiasm.
Many people judge a religion by its art, and why indeed
shouldn't they? And if a particular sect or creed is producing poetry which is far below the standard of the non-
religious verse that is being written at the same time, then
there is surely something wrong with that religion. In the
case of Catholicism, there is something wrong with the state
of the Church (and we too often forget that the Church is
a body of *people*), if all it can produce is plaster, effeminate
Sacred Heart statues and tinkling, doggerel hymns.

   R. S. Thomas, in his useful *Penguin Book of Religious
Verse*, asks in his Introduction: "What is the common
ground between religion and poetry? Is there such? Do
definitions help? If I say that religion is the total response
of the whole person to reality, but poetry the response of
a certain kind of person, I appear to be doing so at the
expense of poetry...." He goes on to invoke Coleridge's

theory of the Primary and Secondary Imagination and so moves slightly away from the subject which, at the moment, I have in hand.

A Catholic (though this book is not only dealing with poets who were Catholics) would, of course, have to be rather more explicit than Thomas is; we are not accustomed to speak of reality but of God who is the only Reality. Nevertheless, he makes some important and relevant points. So also C. S. Lewis, in his last and posthumously published book, *The Discarded Image*, when he declares, "If we had asked Boethius why his book contained philosophical rather than religious consolations, I do not doubt that he would have answered, 'But did you not read my title? I wrote philosophically, not religiously, because I had chosen the consolations of philosophy, not those of religion, as my subject. You might as well ask why a book on arithmetic does not use geometrical methods.'"

I quote this here in order to stress the fact that if a man is a Christian and writes poetry, we almost automatically label him "a Christian poet", as though we expected everything he wrote either to be didactic or moralizing. "Christian poet" has much less meaning than, say, "country poet", or "tragic poet", where we are referring to a specific *subject-matter*; Christian poets can use any subject-matter. It is the *attitude* of so-called Christian poets which is Christian, and there can be a thousand different ways of demonstrating such an attitude. When—to take a few names at random—we look at Chaucer, Milton, Dryden, Coventry Patmore, Hopkins and Eliot, we can see at once how complex the question of actually being a "Christian poet" is. On the surface, these men would appear to have little in common. Hopkins is completely idiosyncratic, while the work of the other poets in this group could hardly be said to contain a single quality which can be pointed to at once by the critic and identified as the Christian element.

In earlier times, of course, particularly in the Middle Ages, English poetry took Christianity for granted, both as its background and living spirit. For all that, poets seldom felt limited by their creed; we have only to recall Chaucer ridiculing the selling of Indulgences in *The Canterbury Tales* to know this. Nevertheless, the nineteenth century and even more, the twentieth *have* complicated matters for poets. When one thinks, for example, of Eliot and of the young Jesuit poet Peter Levi we see how the first (when he was converted to Anglicanism) took Christian themes as his subject-matter, in *Ash Wednesday* and *The Four Quartets*, while the second is often scarcely recognizable at all as what we commonly think of when we consider the phrase "Christian poet" or "Catholic poet". In other words—and this would seem to be an obvious point—poets today who are practising Christians are as unlike each other, as individuals, as any other contemporary poets. Christianity does not colour their work to such an extent that the label "Christian" marks them off at once from their contemporaries. If their religion is truly a part of their lives, the informing spirit of their work, it does not follow automatically that they will always be writing about their faith or their religious experiences, but rather that Christianity will be to their writing what existentialism, or even Communism, or love, or a love of the country, will be to another poet. A statement like this may shock some pious readers, but there is really nothing shocking about it.

If we live fully in the contemporary world, we must learn to accept the fact that to be a poet at this time is to be something of an anomaly. I do not mean that Christian poets today must, on the one hand, flaunt their religious beliefs or, on the other, water it down so that it is as neutral and unnoticeable to readers as possible. Yet neither must the poet who happens to be a Christian betray his art by using it simply as a medium for the propagation of articles of the Faith nor, even more naïvely, attempt to use it as an instrument for conversion. There is a poetic morality as well as a religious one, and every poet is bound by the first, even if not by the second.

In previous ages, such problems as these did not arise. It was really only with the Reformation, when men became freer in their ideas, that their poetry also expressed unrest about their art. For if a poem does not contain the whole man, it might as well not exist at all. But I shall return to this matter later, when I must, of necessity, give some sort of historical survey of the growth of Christian poetry.

The vital question we must now ask is: In what way does Christian poetry differ in kind from secular poetry, or does it not really differ in kind at all? Briefly, is subject-matter—the Christian creed and the poet's reaction to it—the only way in which we can distinguish Christian from other poems? I am inclined to think so, since poetry, whether its content and the belief of its writer be Christian, pagan, or whatever one likes to conceive, is a unique art form, and it must obey its own rules; I would even go so far as to say that subject-matter is by no means its most important feature. The *treatment* of subject-matter, integrity, truth, technical skill, rhythmical dexterity—these qualities are essential if a poem is to be good or even interesting.

Through the centuries we shall find that Christian poetry has differed in the quantity of its didacticism and the quantity and quality of its purely poetic value. Such poetry cannot afford to cheapen or impoverish itself by relying on grandiose themes, and ignore aesthetic standards, in order to do, as it thinks, justice to itself. It must obey the disciplines of *all* poetry; and it is unfortunately only too often that readers of it are willing to overlook the poverty of its skill merely because they believe the doctrines which a particular hymn or verse-form enshrines.

Thus we come to the subject of hymns. They are, or were, written to be sung certainly, and therefore have only a subordinate part to play. Music and worship come first, words are merely part of the worship. Yet the best hymn-writers—like the best writers of libretti—have realized that a muffled gibberish is neither worship nor poetry. Probably the best comparatively modern hymn-writers in English (I am not now speaking of the Middle Ages or slightly later times) were Penn and Newman. Each recognized the fact that the words must not entirely override the music, and that words were prayers set to the best music available. On the whole, however, we are bound to conclude that a considerable number of hymns are not really worth the name of poetry. I am speaking of metrical language, not of words linked with music, an art with totally different rules of its own. But we also have to remember that, in one sense, a badly sung Mass, a squeaking harmonium and an ugly church do not invalidate the truth of the religion they are expressing. Let us not forget, though, that we go to church to see and offer to God the best and most beautiful art forms we can discover and make. Aesthetics, I would firmly maintain, *does* enter into Christianity, and it is an insult, though not a culpable one, to offer God a form of worship which has far less expertise and skill than the secular art of the same period. This is a particularly modern problem, since in the Middle Ages, and even later, almost all art sprang from religion; they were arts and crafts too. That is to say, the anonymous artists of Chartres were working together, each man producing part of a whole. All *believed* in the value of what they were doing, even if all were sinners to some degree or other.

With the Reformation and later, things became more

complicated. Poetry became more and more personal, more and more inward. Though it is true that the earliest English drama sprang from the Church itself, it soon became a purely secular form of its own. And where men had written a poetry of strict conformity, they soon, even if they were Catholics, began to write poems which expressed not the great truths and dogmas of Christianity, but their own feelings about these things. And in the seventeenth century, of course, poets like Donne and, in the nineteenth, men like Hopkins made religious conflict, and even doubt and self-questioning, the very subject-matter of their verse; yet no one could deny that such a poetry was truly Christian. In a sense, it was more deeply Christian than the anthems and hymns of earlier times, since it arose entirely from the depths of the poet's own feelings and ideas. Naïveté was often lost, but the sort of sophistication that can issue from Donne's

> From the round earth's imagined corners blow
> Your trumpets, angels . . . ,

or from Hopkins'

> Wert thou my enemy, though my friend,
> How wouldst thou worse, I wonder, than thou dost
> Defeat, thwart me?

—this sort of sophistication was ample recompense, a real development.

Religious poetry has thus become a personal relationship between man and God. Awe and reverence have not been lost; it is only an unthinking acceptance or a sense of the remoteness between man and his Creator which has disappeared. The simplicity of some Anglo-Saxon and medieval poetry has remained, but something else has been added. I mean that truth to nature, that freshness and integrity which all valuable poetry possesses. That poetry can also be labelled "Christian" does not, perhaps, have a great deal to do with the matter. A remark like this may sound like heresy, but nevertheless, I believe it to be profoundly true. No amount of good will or orthodox belief in the world ever managed to produce a good poem. With regard to Christianity, this is a point which needs to be stressed over and over again. So much prejudice and predilection are attached to the subject; so much conservatism too. We should remember what Pope Paul VI said when he was Archbishop of Milan: "You cannot ... solve the problems of the twentieth century with the mentality of the nineteenth" (or, I might add, of the fourteenth, fifteenth, sixteenth, seventeenth, or eighteenth) "... (an earlier Pope) used the 1st of May as an illustration that here was something which the Church had taken and baptized, associating it with St Joseph, not in order in any way to weaken its human and social significance, but to crown that significance with a religious significance as well, *because human and social aspirations are things good in themselves* (italics mine) and only bad when they are placed over against the Church, and used as an argument against the Christian faith."

I am not simply taking some remarks of the Holy Father out of their context and applying them to a very different subject. I am quoting them because they seem to me to apply to art as well as to politics. Pope Paul is willing to see and admit how things must change, how old ideas have to be adapted, and this applies as much to the making of a poem as to anything else. One has heard people either praise or blame the apparent changelessness of Chinese poetry and painting, as though changelessness were in itself a virtue. It is not a virtue; it is a denial of something deeply human about mankind. Man must change because his element is time. He has not, is not meant to, enter eternity yet. As Eliot has said,

Only in time, time is conquered.

Poetry, therefore, like all other living art forms, must change as man's knowledge changes, as his scientific discoveries become fuller. Poetry, since its medium is words, is especially involved in all this. I am not talking of anything so naïve as the necessity for a poetry which incorporates self-consciously into language new, long scientific words and unfamiliar phrases; to suggest this would be, or is, as stupid as to try to call a poem religious simply because it mentions dogmas or anything to do with faith and morals.

No, I mean that poetry cannot stand still, and that Christian poems should be as movable and flexible as any other poetry. The ideas and prejudices we have to fight are primarily this wrong-headed notion that poetry with the label Christian attached to it is somehow different from any other kind of poetry. I cannot agree with Auden when he says, in an essay on art and Christianity, in *The Dyer's Hand*, "The Incarnation, the coming of Christ in the form of a servant who cannot be recognized by the eye of flesh and blood, but only by the eye of faith, puts an end to all claims of the imagination to be the faculty which decides what is truly sacred and what is profane." He also declares that the making of a poem is primarily a religious activity, and says, "The impulse to create a work of art is felt when, in certain persons, the passive awe provoked by sacred beings or events is transformed into a desire to express that awe in a rite of worship or homage, and to be fit homage, this rite must be beautiful."

I think that I should disagree with Auden's fascinating points on two counts. Firstly, I cannot agree that Christ's

Incarnation has so enormously affected poetry as to invalidate its main faculty, the imagination. On the contrary, the humanization of art, the art of personal experience, may well be a development from the Redemption and Crucifixion. Where once (in many cultures and many religions) religious verse was indeed the general expression of awe and wonder which poets felt but could not account for, they now have, in Christianity, not only a whole new subject-matter but also an intimacy towards their art which is quite new. Similarly, with the second point Auden makes, although I agree in general that *all* good acts are a turning towards and an offering to God, I cannot see that poetry has any special *rôle* to do this. Certainly, when art (spoken, sung or painted) was a definite part of a particular rite or liturgy (one thinks particularly of the Byzantine Mass and the oral tradition of poetry), then it *was* a special kind of art— perhaps, indeed, the only kind which we can truly call religious.

With the modern liturgical movement, with, in certain quarters, a demand for the vernacular and not Latin even for the most sacred parts of the Mass, we may find ourselves in the interesting position of having to find good writers of personal poetry who are also so moved by the Church's liturgy that they are eager to humanize, by means of language, what in the distant past had always been hieratic, remote and impersonal.

All this seems very much to the point in any discussion of religious poetry, especially at a time when the different sects are, as never before, trying to find points of contact. One must not, however, forget that, from about the sixteenth century onwards, Christianity has always had both a public and a private life—just as most poetry has. Today, the public kind (the ode of celebration and so on) has almost ceased to exist, but that is because such verse has become associated with insincerity. The audiences for poetry now may have shrunk (the only exception is Yevtu-shenko, the young Russian poet, whose very personal poems are enjoyed in book-form and read aloud to thousands of people), but at least the people who do read poetry today, whether it is Christian or otherwise, read it because they *want* to. The true oral tradition has, of course, vanished completely with the arrival of radio, television and other swift and mechanical media of communication. Perhaps we forget, too, that in its day the invention of wireless was as world-shattering as the television set has been in our own time. And, it goes without saying, poetry has been affected by all such developments.

In what way, then, does Christian verse really differ from other forms of the art? Only, I believe, in the attitude and subject-matter of the poet himself. Many critics tend to think that a poet who is a Christian is somehow limited by his religion, that a secret censor is always gazing over his shoulder with threats of the Index and excommunication.

In this book we shall be studying a number of poets from various centuries; what I think we shall find is that they are all very individual and also possessed of a great sense of liberty. Mostly, we shall not feel that their subjects were thrust upon them entirely against their will, and, in any case, when this happened, the poet has always still retained his private treatment, his own attitude. To put the matter rather crudely, he can always get his own back; it is not only painters and sculptors who have included their private ideas or even private jokes in a commissioned work of art.

It is important, too, to stress that one or two very great poets—I mean Keats, Wordsworth and Browning—are so deeply, if not orthodoxly, Christian in their attitude towards life that it would be absurd to omit at least some reference to them. When I am dealing with the nineteenth century, I propose, therefore, to say something about these writers, not so much to give a rather dry exposition of their own

particular philosophies and to indicate where they differ
from Christian orthodoxy but rather to show how deeply
Christian thought has penetrated into the very life of English poetry. One could almost go so far as to say that it is
as truly present in some of the "Beat" poets—especially
in Gregory Corso—as in Herbert or Chaucer. For Christianity, it must never be forgotten, is a matter of the heart
as well as the mind. We are entreated to "love God with
our whole heart, our whole soul and our whole mind".
And the very making of a poem has three qualities in
common with the Christian life; it must spring from the
whole person, not simply from the intellect or the heart.
But a Christian poet has also a rather special vocation.
All making is a small participation in the divine and un-
ceasing act of creation; and this is true whether the poet
is aware of it or not. Indeed, all poets are doing this, but
Christians *know* that they are. In a later chapter, we shall
examine what David Jones, the Catholic poet and painter,
has written specifically on this matter.

To attempt this book is a bold act; perhaps it is an act of
folly. I have certainly begun to wonder about this when
I have sought out, in libraries and book-shops, books on
the same subject or allied subjects, and found virtually
nothing. Yet surely it is a subject that *demands* scrutiny.
Catholics at least cannot go on complacently accepting
sentimental hymns and prayers and accepting them as
poetry simply because they are hallowed by childhood
memories or the perfect orthodoxy of their treatment and
subject-matter. Truth has many ways of appearing and it
is the artist's task firstly to know and love his craft, and
then to manifest complete integrity both to the religion
he believes in and the way in which it moves within himself
and asks for expression.

The last few paragraphs may vex the reader. He or she
may think, "Oh, this book is just going to be another

series of generalizations. It is going to try to prove that *all* English poetry is, at some level or to some degree, Christian." Now this is not my intention at all. My wish is certainly to be inclusive, rather than rigidly exclusive, but I certainly have no desire to prove that poets have really been writing in a Christian tradition from Anglo-Saxon times until the present day. This would be utter nonsense. But, on the other hand, I am not prepared to accept as poetry, say, the weaker verses of Patmore, Belloc or Francis Thompson, simply because these men were Christians. I believe that at the Reformation something was both lost and found by English verse. It will be one of the subjects of this book to substantiate this claim, even though it will have to be done very briefly.

CHAPTER II

ANGLO-SAXON POETRY

Old English, or what is usually described by scholars and students as Anglo-Saxon, is that body of verse in the vernacular which was produced from the seventh century to the Norman Conquest. This is a period which has, I believe, been too often regarded merely linguistically or historically, with the result that its literary and poetic value have been very much neglected. One has to remember, of course, that early English is virtually a foreign tongue to us today; even Chaucer, Langland and the poem *Sir Gawain* (in the Middle English period) need a good deal of glossing and annotating. But, as W. P. Ker has said, "It is always necessary to remember how little we know of Anglo-Saxon poetry and generally of the ideas and imaginations of the Early English. The gravity and dignity of most of their poetical works are unquestionable; but one ought not to suppose that we know all the varieties of their poetical taste."

The greatest mistake which can be made in any examination of the best poems of this period is to suppose that they were rough, crude or childish. Their anonymous authors were highly skilled, sophisticated, and whether they were writing poems of war, riddles or devotional pieces, used the most subtle and difficult balanced, alliterative forms.

On the whole, we have a rich body of Anglo-Saxon verse. As it is obviously impossible to consider it all here,

I shall restrict myself in the main to those poems which deal with specifically Christian themes. The most famous—and rightly famous—are *The Dream of the Rood, The Fall of the Angels, Some Riddles* and a number of Advent lyrics. It is essential to remember, however, that *all* Anglo-Saxon verse was imbued with the Christian spirit. Christianity, in other words, was taken for granted. Religious faith was not a background to the poetry, but if not actually its subject-matter, then always implicitly present and felt. We can, indeed, go so far as to say that questions of aesthetics scarcely arose with such literature: questions of style and mood, yes, but not questions of the meaning of art. Just as a mason carving a cross would not have dreamt of questioning the tradition of the manner in which he was working, still less would he have inquired what art, or the act of making something, actually signified. It is true, of course, that for centuries philosophers in many countries *had* been discussing such issues, but seldom the artists themselves. It was only later that men like da Vinci and Michelangelo both used and questioned their own genius. Philosophizing about such matters was essentially a Renaissance activity.

If the Anglo-Saxon poets were simple and accepting in their attitude to their art, that is the only way in which they were simple. It never occurred to them that their poems were often dealing with the most abstruse theological matters. Yet there is none the less subtlety of conception as well as deep devotion in these lines, spoken by Christ's Cross, in *The Dream of the Rood*:

> When the Hero clasped me, I trembled in terror,
> But I dared not bow me   nor bend to earth.
> ......I was wet with blood
> From the Hero's side   when he sent forth his spirit.

There is another very remarkable passage, which mingles

imagination with the spirit of prayer, in a less famous poem
entitled *The Ascension*:

> It was the first leap   when our Lord descended
> To the spotless Virgin,   and free of sin
> Took human flesh.   That came for a comfort
> To all the dwellers   over all the earth.
> It was the second leap   when the Babe was born
> Cradled in a manger   in swaddling clothes,
> The glory of all glories   in the guise of a child.
> It was the third leap   when the Lord of heaven,
> The Father, the Comforter,   mounted the Cross.

Much of the material which the Anglo-Saxon poets used
was readily available—that is to say, in Scripture and the
liturgy. It would be false, however, to suggest that these
poets *only* selected Christian themes; they often wrote of
old legends and heroic stories which had for a long time
played a large part in the life of their imaginations. What
makes their Christian verse so fascinating, though, is the
ease with which they wrote about their religion; they
obviously *felt* it personally, but it was a long time before
such verse could be expressed as personally as, for example,
love or the fear of death.

It must be admitted that there is much that is alien
to us in Anglo-Saxon poetry—its literalness, its insistence
on allegory, its love of riddles, the occasional monotony
of its alliteration. On the other hand, many readers find
it more interesting and sympathetic than Middle English
poetry. This is probably partly because the latter is often
extremely naïve in conception, and is also written in a
language which is definitely in an interim stage. This last
point, I think, makes us tend to judge it as we should judge
a much more modern poem. Consequently, we often mis-
conceive both its meaning and purpose.

Thus the oral tradition of early English poetry started
firstly as a concern with the crafts of poetry, and then with

the meaning of the poem in question. Today it is difficult for us not to see the choice by poets, of specific religious subjects, as an over-conscious, rather artificial thing. We forget that the sacraments, the Mass, the Bible, were as full of meaning to poets who were writing before the Norman Conquest as our own individual and very personal experiences are to poets of our own time. This holds true even when we remember the obsession of the Anglo-Saxons with history, heroism, allegory, riddle-making, bestiaries and battles. Everything their poets saw and felt could be included and celebrated in verse; nothing was too grand or too humble.

The Anglo-Saxon poets were great riddle-makers; they took immense pleasure both in the play of words and in the play of wits, and this, contrary to the superficial conception, is a highly sophisticated art. It is the sort of thing we usually find when an art is highly developed, not when it is in its infancy. And of course it is true that Anglo-Saxon poetry, the first real *English* poetry, does not seem to have had to go through many of the rough, crude, childish phases such as many of the other arts have had to undergo (a fact which a number of the eighteenth-century critics failed to see). But then our vernacular poetry had a strong Latin tradition on which to lean; it did not spring out of the air of its own volition. Here are some examples of the riddles; unlike the gnomic verses, they have only a very gentle moral flavour—hence, perhaps, their charm and wit. Here is *Riddle on the Bookworm*:

> A moth ate words. That seemed to be
> A curious matter when the wonder dawned on me,
> That a grub could eat up the words of a man,
> A thief in the dark his teaching and plan,
> And the stealthy guest
> Would be no wiser for his eating of the nest.

And here is the ending of *Riddle on Moon and Sun*:

> ......Dew came down.
> The night followed after. But never a man
> Knew where the wandering thing had gone.

Early English poetry in the vernacular seldom bores with too much allegory or too much moralizing; yet neither is it naïve. The less interesting Middle English poetry was often to sink into a tired versification of platitudes. This seldom happened in Anglo-Saxon.

One very large question arises when one is considering this very early Christian verse. Is one to regard it as a foreign tongue? It is difficult to give a swift and absolute answer to such a question. Maybe one can only say that for the non-scholar, the average reader of poetry, it *is* a foreign language; it simply cannot be read without grammars, dictionaries and even translations.

In his splendid lecture. "Beowulf, the Monsters and the Critics", the great writer and Anglo-Saxon scholar Professor Tolkien has probably said the wisest and most valuable things about Anglo-Saxon poetry: here, there is only space to quote what seem to be his most important comments (it should be added that what Tolkien says about *Beowulf* may well be applied to the other poems which are being considered in this chapter):

> In England this imagination (the Norse imagination) was brought into touch with Christendom, and with the Scriptures. The process of "conversion" was a long one, but some of its effects were doubtless immediate: an alchemy of change (producing ultimately the medieval) was at once at work. One does not have to wait until all the native traditions of the olden world have been replaced or forgotten; for the minds which still retain them are changed, and the memories viewed in a different perspective: *at once they become more ancient and remote, and in a sense darker.*

This dark side of the Anglo-Saxon imagination is something which must never be ignored or neglected in any true reading of early English poetry. We come upon it most poignantly and vividly in, for example, *The Fall of the Angels*:

> I cannot now conceive   how I sank thus low
> Into this steep abyss,   stained with my sins,
> Cast out from the world.   But well I know
> That he shall for ever be banished   from eternal bliss
> Who planneth not to obey   the Prince of Heaven
> And to please the Lord.

Something must certainly be said about the *Advent Lyrics*, which appear in the manuscript Chapter I and illustrate some of the most direct and passionate Anglo-Saxon verse in existence. In these lyrics, the familiar habit of alliteration is, I think, particularly effective:

> O Rising Sun!   Most radiant angel
> Over the middle-earth   sent unto men!
> Thou steadfast flow   and gleaming of the sun
> Bright beyond stars!   Thou from Thyself
> Dost illumine with light   the time of every season
> As Thou wast once begotten   God of God,
> True son of the Father   before all ages
> For ever Lord   in celestial light....

And in the *Ascension* poem, from a later part of the *Christ* manuscript, we discover the same directness, the same simple and ecstatic approach to our Lord both as God and man:

> Then suddenly in air   came a rush of sound,
> A host of heaven's angels,   a beauteous bright band,
> Messengers of glory,   in gathering throngs,
> Our King rose up   through the temple's roof,
> Where the gathering throng   of his chosen thanes
> Remained on earth   in their place of meeting.
> They saw their Lord   ascend on high,
> Their God from the ground....

As W. P. Ker asserts, quoting what Milton said about his own blank verse, "the sense (is) variously drawn out from one line to another". Ker himself continues, "The Anglo-Saxon poets, at their best, are eloquent, and able to carry on for long periods without monotony. Their verse does not fall into detached and separate lines. This habit is another evidence of the long culture; Anglo-Saxon poetry, such as we know it, is at the end of its progress"; hence, what we can only call the ripeness and maturity of this period of English. It is strange indeed that critics, as they certainly have done, should have so often regarded it as crude or primitive.

There is no doubt about the difficulty of Early English verse; it presents formal problems as well as a language barrier. Yet, for all that, its religious spirit is essentially English—strict, direct, undemonstrative and deeply sincere; it leads straight into the work of Herbert, Vaughan and, much later, Hopkins. It is odd, yes, but not alien.

This earliest period of poetry in the vernacular is often considered in the wrong light; indeed the same thing has also sometimes happened with Middle English and the Middle Ages in general. Some historians and critics have either attempted to throw a false glow of glamour over the art of these centuries, or else to present them as uncouth, illiterate and without artistic skill. Both views are grossly false, though it is, perhaps, less dangerous to over-romanticize the past than to be patronizing about it. One is reminded of T. S. Eliot's curt remark when someone, speaking of classical literature, said to him that, "We know so much more than they did." Eliot replied, "Precisely, they are that which we know."

It is also essential to bear in mind another quite different point; W. P. Ker has put it very well: "The new learning did not always discourage the old native kind of poetry. Had that been the case, we should hardly have had anything like *Beowulf*; we should not have had the poem of Maldon (*The Battle of Maldon*). Christianity and Christian literature did not always banish the old-fashioned heroes." And why, indeed, we may well ask, should they have been expected to? Christianity has always had an especial gift for combining the old with the new, for blending the ancient culture with the unfamiliar dogma, hence, of course, its missionary success.

But the question is really much bigger than that. What touches on poetry and art also affects the whole of life, and if, as most critics would agree, Christianity, with its concrete dogma of the Incarnation, its mingling of the human and the divine, is especially suitable to artistic expression—this is as much due to the nature of the religion itself as to any aesthetic theories or particular artistic skills. Art is a potent thing and it is easy to see why the Puritans banished statues and all forms of decoration from their places of worship. But the Church herself, though unintentionally and unwittingly, has often produced scandal by permitting the use of cheap doggerel (called, hopefully, hymns), and statues of the Sacred Heart which, as Graham Greene remarked in one of his plays, owe a good deal to the lurid illustrations in medical books.

But to return to the question of art and the Incarnation. As we have seen already, W. H. Auden has expressed the view (a view which will be examined in more detail in the concluding chapter) that the Incarnation has, in fact, made a truly Christian art virtually impossible, partly because he thinks that it has banished the mysterious and numinous in religion, and also for more subtle reasons. Myself, I think that he is quite wrong. Christ's death and resurrection, and his whole working, teaching life, have provided a subject-matter for art and literature which can probably only be rivalled in Mohammedanism. For subject-matter is more than mere support or scaffolding; it is a defence against the abstract. In Early Christian Literature, we find no abstractions; even the riddles and the didactic sections of poems are well supported by allegory or anecdote, and the allegory is still lively, not yet mechanical or moribund. It reaches its heights in later centuries, it is true, and is particularly remarkable in Chaucer and Langland, but we can undoubtedly trace its real beginnings back to Anglo-Saxon verse.

In this chapter, it has been necessary to restrict myself, for reasons of space, to poems which are specifically Christian in subject-matter. This seems to have been the most sensible way to handle a body of verse which is, after all, essentially concerned with Christian themes. I should not, however, like to give a false picture of the literature of the period. One must not forget the battle poems, the heroic ones and the bestiaries. Perhaps an example from one of the last-mentioned will show how a beast or bird poem could sometimes be employed for religious ends. *The Phoenix* is one of the best examples of this genre:

> ... from near and far
> He gleans and gathers   to his lodging-place
> Pleasant plants   and fruits of the forest,
> All sweetest spices   and fragrant herbs
> Which the King of glory,   Lord of beginnings,
> Created on earth   for a blessing to men,
> The sweetest under heaven.

And the poem continues,

> Then from that country   the Phoenix flies
> To seek his homeland,   his ancient seat.
> He wings his way   observed of men
> Assembled together   from south and north,
> From east and west,   in hurrying nests.

We should notice, I think, how observant and careful these Anglo-Saxon poets were. There may have been a common language and poetic convention within which all of them worked, but none seems to have felt fettered or restricted by the poetic habits of his own time.

Anglo-Saxon verse was an end and a beginning—the beginning of vernacular verse as the common language of poets, and also the end of a kind of perfection which only the blending of sophistication and simplicity can ever achieve in any art. It was an end too (to a great extent) of anonymity as a presiding factor in poetry. The poets after the Norman Conquest, and especially the great ones, like Chaucer and Langland, who appeared in the fourteenth century, were essentially *individuals*, and in this, if in nothing else, they were modern poets. I think this is an important, and often ignored, truth.

CHAPTER III

MIDDLE ENGLISH POETRY

In this chapter, I shall discuss mainly Chaucer, Langland, Gower, *The Pearl* and *Sir Gawain*. Most space will be devoted to the first three poets, since they offer more to the critic who wants to illustrate the richness of Middle English poetry.

Sir Gawain, none the less, is regarded by Brian Stone, who has recently made a translation of the poem, as "the masterpiece of medieval alliterative poetry ...". He goes on to show how very different it is from any of Chaucer's verse, and points out:

> the successful way in which the poet has subordinated the French courtliness to its place in an English setting that convinces ... of the originality of the work.... We must turn to *Sir Gawain* ... as to a poem in which a Christian knight's courage, good faith, courtesy, and chastity ... are celebrated, to the glory of the House of Arthur and the Britain which thought of Arthur as its first great hero. *It is above all a Christian poem* [italics mine] on the one hand extolling the temporal and spiritual joys of the season and the society which expressed them, and on the other representing marvellous adventures in the world of dark terror that all knew to exist behind their hospitable castle.

This last is well said, and expresses that odd mixture of joy and terror which we seem to find in most Christian poetry which was written before the Reformation, before men had put absolute faith in Christ and the Incarnation, and when they looked back to the Dark Ages, still so close, in which people lived in a world of many strange ideas and many uncertainties. With the conversion of Britain to Christianity, many of the old ideas lingered on in half-concealed and frightening forms (many superstitions and so on), but the new bright certainty filled most men's lives with joy and light.

Perhaps at this point one ought to say something about the medieval concept of courtly love, that profane love, where the lover was at the mercy of every whim of his mistress. As Nevil Coghill has said, such a notion is quite at odds with the idea of Christian marriage, and could not, therefore, without some curious bending of the conscience, exist alongside it. But in many cases it did, although only among members of the aristocracy who had the leisure and inclination to play this particular game of love.

However, it is not for this or, indeed, for its allegory or religious feeling that *Sir Gawain* is most notable. It seems to me that its great charm and attraction lie in its visual beauty, its brilliant descriptions, its pictures of hunts and courts. But this beauty is never static. Though it has the kind of vivid simplicity such as we find in a picture like Uccello's *Hunt by Night*, its rhythm and movement are as essential to the spell it casts upon us as its precision, form and colour.

> Finally by the fireside in a fair room they sat,
> And chamberlains brought the chevaliers choice wines,
> And in their jolly jesting they jointly agreed
> On a settlement similar to the preceding one....
> Bugles blew the triumph, horns blared loud.
> There was hallooing on high by all those present;

. . . .

> Then one who was wise in woodcrafts
> Started in style to slash open the boar.

Although so much of *Sir Gawain* is a poem of action and adventure, it is also a romance of the most delicate kind:

> Gawain spoke his gratitude, they gravely embraced,
> And sat in serious mood the whole service through.
> Then the lady had a longing to look on the knight;
> With her bevy of beauties she abandoned her pew.
> Most beautiful of body and bright of complexion,
> Most winsome in ways of all women alive. . . .

The gallantry, the excessive flattery and romanticism have taken us easily into the world of Gower's *Confessio Amantis*, though the romantic content in the latter poem is much stronger than that of Langland, say. One ought to add, however, that even the most acute critics have often dismissed Anglo-Saxon, and Middle English Literature too, as of little interest; Rose Macaulay was such a critic, and even the more scholarly Douglas Bush declares (speaking of Chaucer and Langland): "The *Vision* is a work of art, in design and in details, and it contains passages of a kind quite beyond Chaucer's reach; yet it remains for us, a sombre signpost rather than a poetic possession." As for the poetic Arthurian romances, Bush has little time for them. But surely those who neglect, or are condescending to Old and Middle English, not only show a deep gap in their own imaginations, but also miss a great deal of really fine poetry.

Gower's *Confessio Amantis* is a very fluent poem, which is much concerned with love, and it needs to be since so many readers now are concerned almost exclusively with sensation and sexual sin. The poet's method is semi-dramatic—that is to say, the poem is a highly artificial dialogue between Gower and his confessor, in which the confessor illustrates numerous sins by means of myth and anecdote. Almost inevitably, of course, the poem does at times become monotonous. It is difficult, after all, to sustain a short-length line in such a long poem. In its curious way, the poem is a virtuoso piece, and not only on account of Gower's apparently inexhaustible fluency.

To turn to Chaucer from Gower is rather like moving from Marlowe to Shakespeare. Like Shakespeare, Chaucer presents to us a rich, lively world full of colour, characters and psychological wisdom; whether he is tilting at the Church, as in parts of the Prologue to *The Canterbury Tales*, or writing his great love poem *Troilus and Criseyde* (surely one of the most moving poems about passion ever written), he is never boring or monotonous. He can be serious, humorous, satirical, romantic and a hundred other things. As a Christian, he feels that his faith is tough enough to withstand the fiercest criticism. Thus, in *The Canterbury Tales*, he remarks of a friar:

> A friar there was, a wanton and a merry.
>
> . . . .
>
> He had made full many a marriage
> Of young women at his own costs.
>
> . . . .
>
> Full well beloved and familiar was he
> With franklyns over all in his country,
> And also with worthy women of the town.
>
> . . . .
>
> Full sweetly heard he confession,
> And pleasant was his absolution.

Chaucer's wit is as vivid and sturdy today as it was in the fourteenth century; one always feels, too, that he has a genuine fondness, even perhaps an especial fondness, for his knaves, rascals, rogues and women of the town. Christian charity pervades all that he writes. Chaucer, without any doubt, is one of the very great English poets; his poetic vein is wide and deep. He can move with the utmost ease from the charming, tapestried lyricism of *The Book of the Duchess* and *The Legend of Good Women* to the numerous and diverse *Canterbury Tales* and the marvellously sustained and passionately felt *Troilus and Criseyde*; and the poet has the humility to introduce, towards the end of this last-named poem, a gracious Christian note:

> Repaireth home from worldly vanity,
> And of your heart up casteth your visage
> To thy God that after his image
> Made you. . . .

One could go on at great length about Chaucer as a poet, a Christian and, surprisingly, a man of the world. Yet this last is not perhaps so surprising for a man whose experience of life was so great and varied. Where could Chaucer have learnt his knowledge of human nature, and where could he have met so many types of men and women except in the great world? Yet he is not a worldly writer in the sense, say, that Pope often was; he had deep spiritual feeling and a passionate love for his religion. It was *because* he loved the Church and her teaching so much that he hated the abuses which bad priests and worldly friars practised. It actually hurt him to see so perfect a thing brought into disrepute. But, of course, his criticisms of what sometimes went on in fourteenth-century abbeys were always made from within. Because a few people sold indulgences, this sort of thing did not make Chaucer inveigh against the whole widespread, teaching Church. We sometimes forget, I think, that he was often an idealist both about women and about religion.

To turn now to Langland seems a long step. In fact, it is
not really such a vast one. There is not space here to go into
the difficult matters of disputed texts; we only have space
to examine his long, religious, intense allegorical poem.
"*Piers Plowman* is", as Nevil Coghill has pointed out, "a
Christian poem about humanity, and it deals entirely with
the most important of all questions possible to the
Christian, namely, 'How can a man win salvation?' In
other words, the poem is an inquiry into the nature of the
Good Life, judged by Christian criteria." It is a dream
poem in so far as Langland uses the device of the dream to
indicate William's Vision of Piers, and of Do-well, Do-
better, and Do-best.

Here, then, is a subject almost as ambitious as that of
The Divine Comedy, but it lacks the detail, sophistication
and great sustained passages of beauty of the Italian. Also,
Langland is a much more limited poet than Dante or
Chaucer. The effects he can bring off are sometimes amaz-
ingly moving, but they are moving, generally speaking, on
the level of simplicity. His is a childlike (something very
different from a childish) vision. Indeed, in his dream, Piers
asks (this is a prose version of the poem):

> "What is charity?" I asked him then.
> "A childlike thing," he replied, "for 'unless you become as
> little children, you shall not enter into the kingdom of
> heaven'. It is a frank and generous goodwill, without folly
> or childishness."

Piers Plowman is full of scriptural references and quota-
tions, but they are usually so carefully assimilated into the
whole poem that they seldom become tedious. It is a passionately felt piece, written by a man of intense faith. When
he writes of the temptations which those who possess the
faith often experience, Langland is particularly vivid: "The
Flesh is also a fierce wind, laden with lust and pleasure—a

wind which blows so loud in blossom-time that it breeds
lustful glances and lascivious words, which break out into
evil deeds or worms of sin; and these will eat the blossoms
down to the bare leaves."

At times, Langland appears rather Puritanical, but only,
I believe, if we compare his world with the richer, wider
one of Chaucer. He certainly doesn't lack a sense of
humour or love of nature, while compassion for man is all-
pervasive in his poem.

In considering, although necessarily so briefly, this unusual dream poem, this visionary piece of Early English
literature, one cannot avoid saying something about allegory. In modern times (with, say, a poet like Edwin Muir),
allegory has become a highly complex literary device which
is often used purely subjectively. Langland, on the other
hand, belonged to a religion and a creed with which all his
readers and listeners were completely familiar; he did not
need to elucidate. Paradoxically, it is we today who live
and work within a non-Christian tradition, who need to
have much of Langland's poem explained to us. J. F.
Goodridge, in his prose version of the poem, has declared,
"Langland did not attempt to sustain an illusory dream-
world, like Spenser's *Faerie Queene*. He held up his dreams,
like distorting mirrors, to the real world of human experience, and turned round, from time to time, to address his
audience in person. *His purpose in writing was first to
discover* (italics mine). . . ."

This last sentence shows that Langland, as a person and
a poet, was by no means merely didactic. Religion was his
subject, as love might be that of another poet. This probably is what has kept his poem alive today; *The Vision* is
far more than simply an archaic piece of literature, of
interest mainly to the scholar. It is difficult, certainly, for
a number of reasons, but it is well worth tackling these in
order to discover Langland's many original felicities.

Pearl, a poem which is less famous than *Sir Gawain*, has that dreamlike quality which we find in a number of Anglo-Saxon and Middle English poems; it is a quality that seems to have been lost to English literature by the time of the late fifteenth and early sixteenth century. But, of course, *Pearl* bears many resemblances to *Sir Gawain*, though its strict stanza form does, perhaps, take us forward to Spenser; the author of *Pearl*, however, is nothing like so skilful as the author of *The Faerie Queene* in sustaining the form and the general interests of his poem. The American critic, David M. Zesmer, has called it:

> some sort of religious allegory. For one reader the Pearl symbolizes purity; for another, the Eucharist; a third finds in the experience of the dreamer a parallel to the mystic's emergence from depression, or "spiritual dryness", into a renewed sense of oneness with God. According to a theory which is currently attracting considerable attention and sympathy, the dreamer in the garden is fallen man. The Pearl is equated with his lost innocence that will be eventually restored.... The various symbolic readings, however, need not exclude the possibility that *Pearl ... may have a core of human emotion to provide its driving force* [italics mine]. *Pearl* certainly succeeds artistically on both the personal and allegorical level.

Perhaps to say such things is to make over-ambitious claims for this poem. In his enthusiasm, the critic has forgotten not only the barrier of language but also the difficulty for the modern reader of entering into the world and context of *Pearl*. It is hard enough to interest oneself genuinely in *The Faerie Queene*, and even *Paradise Lost* and *The Prelude* present difficulties (difficulties, it should be said, that have little to do with the mere *length* of these poems). No, I think that it is the allegorical mode of *Pearl* which we suspect and, since we cannot ignore it without missing the poem's many fine qualities, the whole matter becomes a question of asking ourselves if we are willing to take the trouble to read the poem or not. I personally think we lose a valuable experience if we ignore it altogether.

Even if one knows little either of the nature of allegory or of theology, *Pearl* still offers a good deal; its language and rhythm are almost always felicitous and smooth, it manifests a simplicity that should never be mistaken for simplemindedness, and, above all, it has that freshness and vigour which we also find in Chaucer, Langland and Gower. Here, one feels, are the real beginnings of English lyric and narrative poetry. Anglo-Saxon verse can hardly be taken into account in this question, since the linguistic difficulties seem often to be very nearly insuperable. But Middle English, at its best, is undoubtedly the beginning of a great tradition; it is very exciting to see its inception.

CHAPTER IV

THE FIFTEENTH AND SIXTEENTH CENTURIES

The fifteenth century is often regarded as one of the least exciting in English literature. It is unusual for England to have a period which seems so poverty-stricken in the matter of poetry. England is lucky to be one of those countries which has almost consistently gone on, century after century, producing fine lyrics and dramatic or narrative verse. The state of the language does, of course, have a good deal to do with what is often regarded as this dullest period in English poetry. The richness of the fourteenth century, followed by the splendid verse of the sixteenth, makes the fifteenth seem drab indeed. The only poetry which can be taken really seriously in the fifteenth century is the work of the Scottish Chaucerians, Dunbar and Henryson, but there is not, unfortunately, space to consider them in this chapter.

To return to the condition of the language in the sixteenth century—it was still somewhat difficult, though it by no means presented the problems which Anglo-Saxon and Middle and late Middle English presented; but it did not attain the richness and assurance (except in its drama) which we have come to associate with the extreme end of this period and, indeed, with almost the whole seventeenth century. Even C. S. Lewis, a critic notable for his enthusiasm as well as his learning, divided the verse of the sixteenth century into the "drab" and the "golden". Sidney, the "dazzling ... aristocratic ideal", though sincerely Christian and possessed of a most gentle and gallant temperament, wrote rather of "honour", particularly in questions of love, than of more specific Christian ideals. His Arcadian poems and sonnet-sequence, *Astrophel and Stella*, are sometimes more interesting as formal experiments than as original pieces putting forward new ideas; Sidney's idea of honour and virtue are not new. They are admirable but wholly conventional.

Spenser presents, to an extreme degree, the whole problem of allegory in literature. He is the first English poet who really saw its full implications; Chaucer is medieval in comparison. In this matter, Spenser is the first modern poet. When he wrote *The Faerie Queene*, he little knew what he was introducing into English literature. Allegory within allegory (like Chinese boxes), extended allegory, allegory in depth—all these come straight from Spenser. I think that it is no exaggeration to say that what David Jones, for instance, is doing today could be shown to have its true roots in *The Faerie Queene*.

What is allegory, then? In its simplest form, it is a kind of double meaning, or one layer of ideas and images suggesting another. In its most complex form, it presents the ideas without the clues; that is to say, the surface explanation or story is omitted altogether and the reader is left to discover the meanings for himself. Like abstract art, this latter type of the form pares away all that is inessential. The kernel is left, the shell thrown away. The kind of verse that uses this method is probably the most complex which we have today.

Spenser never resorted to this very complex kind of writing, but he did make way for it. In other words, he made it possible for English poets to take over a whole new way of approaching ideas and images; for the potentialities of allegory seem endless, since their use depends largely on the personality and originality of the poet who is using it. And here we come to another important event in our literature which was initiated in the late sixteenth century and reached really new heights with the metaphysical poets of the seventeenth. I mean that poetry could at last become a *private* as well as a public affair. Allegory alone was, of course, not responsible for this. Religious disputation, freer thinking on philosophical matters, the Reformation, new worlds being discovered beyond England, scientific inquiry—all these were also responsible for these great changes. Spenser himself was not a Catholic, and perhaps this gave him a kind of freedom which even Chaucer was denied.

With Spenser and Sidney we are at the heart of humanism, and of the Renaissance, as they appeared in England. There was no sudden upsurge of painting and the other arts but there was, as has been suggested already, an awakening of the idea of man as the centre of the universe, of a powerful being for whom almost anything was possible. This spirit was felt throughout Europe, along, of course, with a decline in that reverence towards Almighty God which was the essential spirit of the Middle Ages. In a sense, however, Sidney is still a noble knight, a medieval; his character and the feeling within his verse represent the spirit of love and courage rather than that of adventure and inquiry.

Spenser has often been called "the poet's poet", mainly, I think, because he had such a powerful interest in poetic form; it must surely be admitted that his desire to experiment with metre and language were sometimes stronger than his concern with subject-matter or the poem as a whole. Yet to accuse him of being a poet in whom only other poets will find interest and pleasure is altogether to misunderstand this much underrated and rather neglected poet. The truth, alas, is that Spenser is seldom read today

except by school-children; he lacks the drama and resonance of Shakespeare and Milton, the romanticism of Keats,
the humour of Chaucer. One has to be instructed in his
methods before one can understand him fully. Also, even
his skill at varying his rhythms or rhymes cannot always be
sustained and, on occasion, his strict stanzas provide hard
work for us, his readers.

If anyone could make Spenser readable and accessible to
"the common reader", it is C. S. Lewis, and this, among
much else that is profound and scholarly, he has done in
his fine book, *The Allegory of Love*. He says, of *The Faerie
Queene*, "... Spenser, while borrowing the Form of the
Italian epic, deliberately modified it by turning it into a
'continued allegory or dark conceit'. He may have been
influenced in this by the allegorical interpretations which
critics had fastened upon Ariosto, and which Tasso, by an
afterthought, was later to fasten on himself. *But the allegory is no afterthought in Spenser's poem*" [italics mine].
When it is allegorical at all it is radically and momentously
allegorical, and continues the medieval impulse whether
under medieval guidance or not. The second answer is
more important. I am trying to tell the history not only of
the form, allegory, but also of the sentiment; and in the
latter story Spenser is not so much part of my subject as
one of my masters or collaborators. The last phase of that
story—the final defeat of courtly love by the romantic
conception of marriage—occupies the third book of *The
Faerie Queene* and much of the fourth. Another interesting
critic, Graham Hough, has put forward the notion that,
although this vast poem was unfinished at Spenser's death,
it nevertheless does have a satisfactory conclusion. I think
this is true. Spenser's purpose throughout the epic is so
obvious that he scarcely needed to make it explicit.

On the face of it, it is odd that *The Faerie Queene* should
so often be given to school-children to read as a set text;

and yet, if one thinks carefully about this apparent anomaly, one can see why. The very fact that *The Faerie Queene* is an allegory means that even a very young child can skim off, as it were, the fable of dragons and princesses and have no need to understand either the concept of courtly love or any deeper philosophical or moral content. Hence, the value and interest of allegory in its earlier stages. To those who are more mature, however, the poem offers layer upon layer of rich meaning—meaning that the poet himself was fully aware of since there is nothing arbitrary about his poem. Spenser knew precisely what he was doing, I think. This is, of course, a matter for dispute, but it seems to me that the poet is "carried away" only in the virtuoso metrical effects of his epic, never in what he wanted to say. He never let his meaning or subject-matter dictate to him. On the other hand, his intricate stanzaic form seems to have got into his blood, so that what seems highly complex to us was most probably an easy affair to him. Most poets, after all, experience this feeling of the form working through them at its own pace and rhythm—when the poem is going well, that is, and written at a fairly high pitch of passion and enthusiasm. There are undoubtedly drab, even dead, moments in a long poem (that is the price a poet has to pay for writing at great length; it is the great heights that sustain him and keep him going).

What, then, is the "grand design" of this long, elaborate poem? It has been called "a romantic epic", and one of its chief purposes seems to be to praise and describe the virtues of Holiness, Chastity, Justice, Courtesy and Mutability; its thinly veiled tribute to Queen Elizabeth (Gloriana) is merely the sort of politeness which poets and other artists practised during the Renaissance. And we must never forget that this *is* a Renaissance poem. It entirely lacks both the simplicity of the Middle Ages and the artificiality of the Baroque. Hazlitt said of Spenser:

"The poet takes and lays us in the lap of a lovelier nature, by the sound of softer streams. . . . He paints nature, not as we *find* it, but as we expected to find it. . . . *The two worlds of reality and of fiction, indeed, seem more distinct than his perceptions* [italics mine]. He is the painter of abstractions."

There are times when this last sentence seems to be entirely true; yet, on the whole, I am inclined to think that Spenser's world is an entirely concrete one. Indeed, were it not so, we, his readers, would not be so convinced and gripped by his allegory and metaphors. Here is an example of what I mean:

> Now gins the goodly frame of Temperance
> Fairly to rise, and her adored head
> To prick of highest praise forth to advance,
> Formerly grounded, and fast setteced [*sic*]
> On firm foundation of true bountihead;
> And this brave knight, that for that virtue fights,
> Now comes to point of that same perilous stead,
> Where Pleasure dwells in sensual delights,
> Mongst thousand dangers, and ten thousand magic nights.

It has often been said that Spenser is better at describing sins and vices than virtues; I cannot altogether agree with such a statement, though it is certainly *always* easier to present sensual matters, since poetry itself works through the senses before it enters the mind. This is a truism and a perfectly orthodox piece of Thomist philosophy. It would not, however, be at all just to say that Spenser gloats on sensual matters—any more than Dante or Milton does.

Having presented Spenser as a kind of moral Romantic, a man of the Renaissance who was not, I think, wholly aware of what true Humanism meant—its questioning and doubts, its near-materialism and its gallantry which often had little to do with religion or charity—we must move on to a much more complex poet.

It is impossible to write a book of this kind and omit the name of Shakespeare. Some critics have thought he was a Catholic, others have decided that he was an agnostic. All the certainty we really have is in the texts of the plays and sonnets. One thing is sure: he was a great Humanist, a great psychologist and a man who loved and understood deeply the springs of human behaviour and character. Nothing seems to have been beyond his comprehension. As Dr Johnson declared, "His story requires Romans and Kings, but he thinks only on men." Shakespeare could be tragic, humorous, farcical, comic, pathetic—and dozens of other things. He understood innocence, as he showed with the children of Macduff, and lust, as he showed with Angelo in *Measure for Measure*. He knew love in its light moods (*Much Ado About Nothing*) and the suffering it can bring about (*Romeo and Juliet*). There is little new to be said about him and yet he is always worth writing about.

But in what sense can Shakespeare be placed in a group of Christian poets? Primarily, on account of his all-embracing charity, I think. He has a compassion for many kinds of men and women which is granted to very few people. And, except in his sonnets, he seldom wrote about himself directly. He looked out on creation and sometimes rejoiced in it, at others was disgusted by it (*Timon of Athens*). Whatever he saw and felt, he never ceased to *care*, and this is surely of first importance in both a Christian and a poet.

With Sidney, Spenser and Shakespeare we reach the apotheosis of English Humanism, the heart of our own Renaissance. What did this mean for Christianity, and for Catholicism in particular? In the first place, it meant that man became aware of a large expanding universe, that his feeling of safety became unsure, that his Catholic Faith was either in jeopardy or else continually questioned—something which, in the long run, comes to the same thing. The

Reformation was not, after all, only the beginning of Protestantism, but also the birth (though the gestation took a long time) of agnosticism and atheism.

How were poets affected by this? I would say that, slowly and almost imperceptibly, their work grew more private, and also more full of inquiries. When we move into the seventeenth century we notice, almost at once, that the greatest of the poets of that period are more cautious, often full of the praise of God, yes, but less carefree than the writers of the Middle Ages or of the fifteenth century. Where Chaucer or Langland, for example, could criticize Christianity, violently sometimes, from *within* the Church, Donne, Herbert and Vaughan were much less concerned with particular religious abuses than with searching their own motives and attitudes. In a word, Christianity became, for the first time, a psychological and personal matter. Poetry went inwards, not outwards. The soul and mind of man were the crucial things. Verse became a battleground where man fought out his problems with God. And it was, I believe, Shakespeare who started the process. His greatest character, Hamlet, is, after all, obsessed by the very problems which beset so many people today—the meaning of life and the difficulty of knowing how to behave in the most extreme and taxing circumstances. Yet, since Shakespeare was incapable of producing mere ciphers for his ideas (in this, the old morality plays have something in common with the most *avant-garde* plays of today—those of Beckett, Pinter and N. F. Simpson), he always puts forward his own perplexities in the form of entirely convincing characters. In his own time he was, I think, unique in this. Ben Jonson, Marlowe and Webster were incapable of creating the subtle characters which Shakespeare invented; they were still too tied to the old idea of the "humours" or else to the representation of the violent or macabre.

As I have suggested already, one can never prove that Shakespeare was a believing or practising Christian; one can only see the qualities in his plays which are essentially Christian in origin—charity, compassion, generosity, forgiveness, and so on. He has been called "myriad-minded", but when one studies his plays with care and thought, one can see how vividly these qualities stand out. There was nothing that Shakespeare could not understand and accept —even his own suffering.

It is in the *Sonnets*, mysterious and often ambiguous as they are, that we come closest to the man himself. Here, the voice that elsewhere hands itself over freely for the use of others, describes the miseries and ecstasies of love and sexual passion. Some of these poems are light-hearted and happy, but many are dark, not with self-pity but with the complexities that men and women discover when this strongest of human instincts holds them within its power. Yet even in these deeply disturbing poems, Shakespeare is often able to view his own feelings and reactions objectively; and surely few poets have written so joyfully of the delight of love as he did when he wrote,

Shall I compare thee to a summer's day . . .?

Seldom was Shakespeare entirely introspective, even in his blackest moods. He possessed self-knowledge to a very remarkable degree, and so was able to comprehend the vagaries of human behaviour in general. There is little that could be more Christian than this.

CHAPTER V

THE SEVENTEENTH CENTURY

The seventeenth century is the richest period in England for religious verse. Even the pious lyrics and plays of the Middle Ages appear not only naïve, but also shallow beside the diversity and individuality of the best poets of the later century. It is not so much that a writer like Donne, for example, stands out among a group of much lesser poets, but rather that he shines as the great star in a galaxy. Without exaggeration, one can say that all the best verse of this time is religious in spirit; and since, with the exception of Crashaw, its finest writers are Protestants, there is a feeling of great freedom about their work. These men are Christians but they are also men. They do not accept the tenets of Christianity unquestioningly. And they are important also because they are the first poets in English who write about religion as a personal experience, rather than as a public offering of praise. The old tradition of almost hymn-like lyricism has been lost, at least for a time, and poetry is Christian in spirit not because to write it is fashionable or acceptable, but because men like Donne, Vaughan, Herbert, Traherne and Crashaw find it the best medium for their inquiries and experiences. It does not, thus, seem surprising to us that after a life of passionate love of women, Donne can turn with perfect ease to God and address his poems to him.

But before we approach these so-called Metaphysicals
(they are really mystical poets), we must also say something
of Milton, the great Christian epic writer of the century
(whatever William Empson may say to the contrary), and
of Dryden, the Catholic forerunner of the poets of the century to come. Yet great as Milton is, resonant as his writing
always appears, and marvellously sustained by incidental
interest as *Paradise Lost* seems, this poet's work somehow
lacks the appeal of a short lyric by Vaughan or Herbert.

In *Paradise Lost*, Milton purports to set out to describe
the period from the Fall of the Angels to the Fall of Man.
Perhaps the epic's most moving felicity is the wonderful
variety of its tone; the poet can move from the vividly
descriptive to the humanly emotional, from the sense of
man's first, innocent relation with God to his shame at his
first sin. One of the reasons for the poem's liveliness is, I
think, its visual interest. But things are tangible as well as
seen. What could have been an abstract treatise is an
exciting and sometimes touching human document; when I
say "touching", I am thinking of those passages at the end
of the poem where Adam and Eve move reluctantly but
with acceptance, out of the Garden of Eden:

> They, hand in hand, with wandering steps and slow
> Through Eden took their solitary way.

This kind of touch is one aspect of Milton's great genius.
The greatest Christian poets—Dante, Chaucer and Shakespeare—have also been capable of the sudden simplicity,
the moment when the great truths are something we can all
recognize in our own lives.

Paradise Regained is a much less interesting poem. For
one thing, Christ himself is made into a most distasteful,
unlovable person. About people, he says:

> By whom to be dispraised were no small praise.

This is not the Jesus Christ of the Gospels who willingly

gathered all manner of men about him, and always had time for everyone. But *Hymn on the Morning of Christ's Nativity* possesses all the qualities which we look for in a truly Christian poet—simplicity, devotion, sincerity and, of course, technical skill.

Dryden was also a Christian and unlike Milton a Catholic, but such a complex one that it is easier to leave him to the end of this chapter than to confuse the reader by bringing him into a discussion of the metaphysical, or mystical, devotional poets. Of all the latter, Donne is the best known and most praised, yet had he not existed at all it is hard to believe that men like Traherne, Herbert, Vaughan, and even Crashaw, would not have received their due as writers. Donne, of course, fascinates us both as a man and a poet. The passionate lover who turns away from human love to a much higher form of it is always of interest, even if that interest is sometimes of the most sensational kind. But Donne wrote in such a way that he arouses in us something much more profound than mere sensationalism. He sometimes addressed God with the passion and violence that he also used towards his mistress, but this only serves to make his religion and religious experience a more intense and alive thing; he had a real relationship with God, as we can see in the following excerpts from his *Divine Poems*:

> Despair behind, and death before doth cast
> Such terror, and my feeble flesh doth waste
> By sin in it, which it t'wards hell doth weigh;
> Only thou art above, and when towards thee
> By thy leave I can look, I rise again.
>
> (*Holy Sonnet I*)

> Death be not proud, though some have called thee
> Mighty and dreadful, for thou art not so.
>
> (*Holy Sonnet X*)

Batter my heart, three person'd God; for you
As yet but knock, breathe, shine, and seek to mend.

(Holy Sonnet XIV)

Apart from the drama in Donne's poems, we also find a directness and intimacy. This, I am sure, is what is new in English Christian poetry. The medieval morality plays and lyrics also possessed simplicity, but it was the simplicity of innocence and even, at times, of naïveté. The metaphysical poets are, on the other hand, almost always extremely sophisticated; their dealings with God are conducted (it may surely be said without blasphemy) on a level where something very like a divine conversation can take place. Helen Gardner, the great authority on Donne, says, "The strength of the religious poetry of the metaphysical poets is that they bring to their praise and prayer and meditation so much experience that is not in itself religious."

This needs to be said, since, almost for the first time in English poetry, man is addressing God with the simple directness of a morality or mystery play, but *also* as an educated man might address (not without awe) his Father and Divine Master. Thus, Donne can write, in *Good Friday, 1613, Riding Westward*:

O Saviour, as thou hangst upon the tree,
I turn my back to thee, but to receive
Corrections, till thy mercies bid thee leave,
O think me worth thine anger, punish me,
Burn off my rusts, and my deformity,
Restore thine Image, so much, by thy grace,
That thou may'st know, and I'll turn my face.

In criticism of seventeenth-century verse much has been made, in modern times, of the use by poets of concrete and tangible imagery. To read some of these critiques, one would almost suppose that there had been no Chaucer and no Shakespeare to do such a thing. Perhaps what such critics mean is that there is a firmness and conviction about the best lyrics of the seventeenth century, a *thinking* through images, which makes religious experience both a very personal and also a very precise and solid thing. T. S. Eliot was the first critic of importance to point this out, but his theory of "the dissociation of sensibility", which he dates back to this century, has surely been made altogether too much of by more recent critics. Eliot felt that, in Donne's time, a real dislocation took place in the minds of poets, with the result that not only did they begin to question their Christian faith, but also began to see all philosophy, metaphysics and art in a totally new light: in a word, mind and heart became separated and worked apart rather than together, the mind and imagination took over what in previous centuries had been done by the whole poet and the whole man.

There is surely much exaggeration in all this; one cannot tie down a change in sensibility so precisely. Nevertheless, Eliot is right when he sees the seventeenth-century attitude towards Christianity (and towards mystical union with God also) as essentially a private matter. There was, indeed, a dislocation not only in the Christian Church as a whole—as a result of the Reformation—but also in men's feelings about and attitude towards dogma and tradition. The love of God, if it meant anything at all, meant something private in each man's soul. And, of course, men cannot live for long without a general and public acceptance of truth. The seventeenth century marks the apotheosis, the flowering-time of private religion; after it came the decline and finally, much later, agnosticism and atheism. This is inevitably a gross over-simplification of a highly complicated matter, but I am sure there is more than a grain of truth in it.

Of all the religious poets of this century, George Herbert

is still the most accessible and sympathetic to us. His manner is straightforward, sometimes a little dramatic even, but his subject-matter and verse forms are handled with such marvellous skill that even the atheist cannot help but admire him. To the Christian, however, he is probably the most satisfying minor poet of the whole seventeenth century; I am prepared to say this without any qualification at all. Let us look at one or two of his finest lyrics:

When God at first made man,
Having a glass of blessings standing by—
Let us (said he) pour on him all we can;
Let the world's riches, which dispersed be,
        Contract into a span.

        .   .   .   .

        Yet let him keep the rest,
But keep them with repining restlessness:
Let him be rich and weary, that at least
If goodness lead him not, yet weariness
        May toss him to my breast.

                                    (*The Pulley*)

What is this strange and uncouth thing,
To make me sigh, and seek, and faint, and die,
Until I had some place where I might sing
    And serve Thee, and not only I,
But all my wealth and family might combine
To set Thy honour up as our design?

    And then, when, after much delay,
Much wrestling, many a combat, this dear end,
So much desired, is given; to take away
    My power to serve Thee; to unbend
All my abilities, my designs confound,
And lay my threatnings bleeding on the ground.

                                    (*The Cross*)

In these poets of the seventeenth century we find not only

a great and very moving intimacy with God but also a psychological truth about religious experience in general and in particular. Vaughan, Crashaw and Herbert have the rare gift of being able to *present* their experiences and examine and analyse them at the same time. In this sense, they lead us directly (and I do not think this is a far-fetched idea) to Browning and the early Eliot. Perhaps this is what T. S. Eliot really meant when he spoke of "dissociation of sensibility".

But, to return to Herbert, there is the beautifully simple close of the famous poem called *Love*:

> "And know you not," says Love, "who bore the blame?"
>> "My dear, then I will serve."
> "You must sit down," says Love, "and taste my meat."
>> So I did sit and eat.

I suppose that this is one of the most exquisitely simple poems in English about Holy Communion. Herbert is not always as direct as this; occasionally his images are rather far-fetched, but very seldom.

Vaughan is as dramatic as Herbert in his approach to God, but his poems, unlike the other poets, tend to express the high-points of mystical experience, rather than the difficult journey to union with God and the personal battles by the way. The fearless nakedness of Vaughan's poems is very remarkable:

> I saw Eternity the other night
> Like a great *Ring* of pure and endless light,
>> All calm, as it was bright,
> And round beneath it, Time in hours, days, years
>> Driv'n by the spheres
> Like a vast shadow moved, . . .
>
> *(The World)*

The experiences which Vaughan transcribes are more

often transcendent than those of Herbert, it is true; he lays
more stress on the evil in man than the latter poet does. But
this does not mean that he is unaware of man's difficulties
and long and troubled searchings for God. We can see this
very well put in the poem called simply *Man*:

> Weighing the steadfastness and state
>   Of some mean things which here below reside,
> Where birds like watchful clocks the noiseless date
>   And intercourse of times divide,
> Where bees at night get home and hive, and flowers
>   Early, as well as late,
> Rise with the sun, and set in the same bowers; ...
>
> He knocks at all doors, strays and roams,
>   Nay hath not so much wit as some stones have
> Which in the darkest nights point to their homes
>   By some hid sense their Maker gave;
> Man is the shuttle, to whose winding quest
>   And passage through these looms
> God ordered motion, but ordained no rest.

What we are most aware of in Vaughan's verse is perhaps
the childlike innocence—an innocence which takes us back
to many of the English fourteenth-century lyrics and
forward to Wordsworth, with his "intimations of immortality". But where Wordsworth, one cannot help feeling,
approaches childhood with a longing which can only arise
from adulthood and a certain amount of sophistication,
Vaughan seems wholly and purely childlike. We must not,
however, confuse innocence with childishness. One only has
to read Vaughan's *The Retreat* to realize that evil and sin
were no strangers to him. This poem is certainly concerned
with innocence, but it is the *loss* of this quality that
Vaughan is really stressing and mourning; he was far too
wise to suppose that a man could grow up without the

knowledge and experience of sin. The poem, in fact, is one of regret and loss, rather than one of celebration:

> Happy those early days! when I
> Shin'd in my angel-infancy.
> Before I understood this place
> Appointed for my second race,
> Or taught my soul to fancy aught
> But a white, celestial thought. . . .
>
> . . . .
>
> Before I taught my tongue to wound
> My conscience with a sinful sound,
> Or had the black art to dispense
> A several sin to every sense,
> But felt through all this fleshly dress
> Bright shoots of everlastingness.
>
> . . . .
>
> Some men a forward motion love,
> But I by backward steps would move,
> And when this dust falls to the urn
> In that state I came return.
>
> *(The Retreat)*

Traherne, the discovery of whose prose and verse seems one of the most unlikely literary phenomena of this century, also shares with Vaughan this combination of a feeling for innocence with a deeply grounded sense of sin. A writer of both poems and the ecstatic prose, *Centuries of Meditations*, Traherne, paradoxically perhaps, seems more poetic in his prose pieces than in his usually rather conventional verse. His prose—especially the *Centuries*—has that wonderful balance, lyricism and careful modulation which we usually expect to find only in poetry. It is as if, for Traherne, the experience of union with God (and there can be little doubt of the genuineness of the experiences he transcribes), could only find true utterance and a faithful expression in a highly wrought yet never overloaded prose. He may at times refer to the Bible, but in general his sources and imagery are all his own, the overflow of the delight he found in his very personal love of God. He is fully aware of the Fall and of sin, yet it is joy and the mercy and sweetness of his Divine Creator that he chiefly celebrates, as for instance, in the famous passage:

> You never enjoy the world aright, till the Sea itself floweth in your veins, till you are clothed with the heavens, and crowned with the stars.... Till your spirit filleth the whole world, and the stars are your jewels; till you are as familiar with the days of God in all Ages as with your walk and table.... Yet further, you never enjoy the world aright, till you so love the beauty of sharing it, that you are covetous and earnest to persuade others to enjoy it.... Can any ingratitude be more damned than that which is fed by benefits? Or folly greater than that which bereaveth us of infinite treasures?

Two things are specially notable about this passage; one is Traherne's complete orthodoxy. There is no suggestion of pantheism in his work; his God is the God who became Man, and Man is capable of holiness because the Incarnation and resurrection actually happened. In the second place, it can never be forgotten or ignored that Traherne was as aware of evil as a poet like Donne, though probably not so deeply acquainted with it personally.

In the *Centuries*, Traherne gives us passages about his childhood which, at times, bear a close resemblance to Vaughan's *Retreat*. I am thinking in particular of the following lines which appear in *The Third Century*: "Will you see the infancy of this sublime and celestial greatness? Those pure and virgin apprehensions I had from the womb, and that divine light wherewith I was born are the best unto this day, wherein I can see the Universe.... Certainly

Adam in Paradise had not more sweet and curious apprehensions of the world, than I when I was a child."

Why, exactly, is it that one feels so absolutely justified in
regarding the *Centuries* as more poetic, more condensed,
more rhythmic, than Traherne's conventional and formal
verse? The main reason, I believe, is that the *Centuries*
possesses a spontaneity which most of the verse altogether
lacks. One is, in fact, reduced to using a phrase which
describes what is still an unpopular poetic form—in other
words, the prose-poem. This form was very unfashionable
indeed five or six years ago, but it seems to be coming back
into fashion. In the seventeenth century, Donne's sermons,
I suppose, fall into this category, but, in modern times, it
is a poetic form which has always been more popular and
accepted abroad than in England; it has always and
everywhere, I think, been regarded as slightly *avant-garde*
and therefore suspect.

Probably Traherne's most famous, and also most beautiful, piece of prose-poetry resides in the following lines:
"The corn was orient and immortal wheat, which never
should be reaped, nor was ever sown. I thought it had stood
from everlasting to everlasting. . . . Eternity was manifest
in the Light of the Day, and something behind everything
appeared: which talked with my expectation and moved my
desire. . . ."

Many lovers of seventeenth-century poetry and prose
find Traherne's the most congenial of all—and I am not
forgetting Donne. The discovery of his work in this century
is one of those happy literary and extraordinary chances
that seldom occur. We are fortunate indeed that his work
should have proved to be such a treasure-house of Christian
mystical literature and so original and refreshing in spirit.

After the simplicity and directness of Traherne (though,
it must be remembered, he is not always nearly so straightforward in his ideas or even in his way of expressing them

as might appear at a cursory reading), the poems of Crashaw often seem cloying and devious. For these reasons, he has never received the acclaim which has been accorded to the other poets I have been talking about. Of them all, it should be noted, he is the only Catholic, so that in one sense at least he was working alone; he did not have that close feeling of sharing and fellowship which his contemporaries must often have been aware of, even though they never worked consciously as a School or Movement of poets; it is we who see them as a group, not they themselves. The labels are applied afterwards, not at the time.

Crashaw's most celebrated poem is his *Memory of St Teresa*; the manner here is elaborate, almost, one might say, baroque, but, nevertheless, genuine religious feeling does penetrate the apparent artificiality:

> O what delight, when she shall stand
> And teach thy lips heaven, with her hand,
> On which thou now may'st to thy wishes
> Heap up thy consecrated kisses!
> What joy shall seize thy soul, when she,
> Bending her blessèd eyes on thee,
> Those second smiles of heaven, shall dart
> Her mild rays through thy melting heart!
>
> Angels, thy old friends, there shall greet thee,
> Glad at their old home now to meet thee.
> All thy good works which went before,
> And waited for thee at the door,
> Shall own thee there; and all in one
> Weave a constellation
> Of crowns, with which the King, thy spouse,
> Shall build up thy triumphal brows.

Crashaw is not one of the most accessible or most popular of the metaphysical poets; his imagery is often too far-fetched and his manner of approach too indirect for him to appeal to the kind of reader who admires Vaughan, Herbert or Traherne. He draws much on the New Testament for his subject-matter, and this tends to give his verse an air of unreality and remoteness to the feelings which he is trying to express. Passion is present in his poems, yes, but it often seems diluted simply because the poet is either too shy or else too awed to present it nakedly. That he *can* be bare, lucid and very simple is abundantly clear from the short poem called *A Song*, which ends:

> Though still I die, I live again;
> Still longing so to be still slain,
> So gainful is such loss of breath,
> I die even in desire to death.

> Still live in me this loving strife
> Of living *Death* or dying *Life*.
> For while thou sweetly slayest me
> Dead to myself, I live in Thee.

When we approach Dryden, we are on the very edge of the eighteenth century; feeling often disguises itself as wit, and it is rare indeed to find an immediate and straightforward reaction either to a religious experience or to the love of God. There is a kind of crisp self-consciousness which often conceals a most delicate and refined sense of the Divine, and which we shall find at its most obvious later in the work of Pope.

Dryden wrote poems, plays and essays; to my mind, his prose is far and away his most lucid and flexible medium— he seems truly to relax in it, to be quite at ease and to have no inhibitions at all. But it is the poems we must consider, and they certainly present one major difficulty; they are often satirical, and it is hard to unite religion and satire. Chaucer managed it, it is true, but he lived at a time when criticizing the Church was almost an essential part of caring for it at all. The situation in the eighteenth-century

Churches was quite different. We shall discover just how different when we study the eighteenth century in the following chapter. Dryden, in a crucial way, bridges the gap between the two periods. He was also—and it is difficult sometimes to believe this—a man of many contradictions: worldly yet shy, a man of many parts, yet a poet of very few themes, and so on. Dr Johnson said of him: "The *Religio Laici*, which borrows its title from the *Religio Medici* of Browne, is almost the only work of Dryden which can be considered as a voluntary effusion; in this, therefore, it might be hoped that the full effulgence of his genius might be found."

We all know that at times Johnson can be an extremely carping and obtuse critic; anyone who has read his brilliant *Preface to Shakespeare*, however, must also realize the genius of his insights, and the purity of his enthusiasm. With Dryden, he takes into account all the most important poems—*Absalom and Achitophel, Mac Flecknoe, The Hind and the Panther*, the numerous translations and prologues, and, what is most relevant here, *Religio Laici*, but he cannot feel real sympathy for this last poem or even be prepared to attempt to lose himself in it. To put the matter mildly, Dr Johnson was a man of firm views, even of violent prejudices. But one only has to read his own fine prayers to realize that he was also a man of deep religious convictions. Perhaps he thought the heroic couplet was too slick a poetic device to be used for a poem which Dryden subtitles *A Layman's Faith*; at all events, after criticizing the poem in no uncertain terms, Johnson does admit: "... nor will it be easy to find another example equally happy of this middle kind of writing, which, though prosaic in some parts, rises to high poetry in others, and neither towers to the skies, nor creeps along the ground."

It is, I think, important to remember when we are considering the whole metaphysical movement that Johnson, in his *Life of Milton*, makes it clear that there were many seventeenth-century poetic innovations which he did not understand at all. A man of high intelligence and great learning, he was not always able to detect what was truly new and valuable in the age just preceding his own. Yet sometimes he was well ahead of his age, and could see felicities and genius which were not obvious to less sensitive and fastidious minds. That he did not give himself totally to an understanding of Dryden may have been in part the fact that the latter was a Catholic convert.

To return to Dryden himself—if we accept the artifices, conceits and conventions of his period we can, I am sure, penetrate to the true religious feeling which resides in a poem such as *Religio Laici* (let us not forget, either, that to write in heroic couplets on so intimate a subject is far more difficult than to invent a verse form or make use of a sonnet); here is Dryden:

> Thus man by his own strength to Heaven would soar:
> And would not be obliged to God for more,
> Vain, wretched Creature, how art thou misled
> To think thy Wit these God-like notions bred!
> These Truths are not the product of the Mind,
> But dropt from Heaven, and of a Nobler kind.
>
> . . . .
>
> Not only Charity bids hope the best,
> But more the great Apostle has exprest:
>
> . . . .
>
> And still the nearer to the spring they go,
> More limpid, more unspoiled, the Waters flow.

It is often hard to believe that Dryden is a seventeenth-century poet at all; his manner is assured, satirical, unquestioning; it lacks the obvious passion of a Donne, or the innocence of a Traherne. Yet it should not, for these reasons, be underrated. It has an admirable, rhythmic flow, and a wonderfully easy yet also highly intelligent approach to almost every subject; it seldom bores with monotony because Dryden himself had such a lively mind. He is not the most sympathetic of the poets we have been considering, but, with the exception of Donne, he is surely the most quick-witted and often the most deep-thinking too.

CHAPTER VI

THE EIGHTEENTH CENTURY

The eighteenth century in England presents religious difficulties which we do not find in the seventeeth, nor even in the troubled period of the Reformation. For one thing, the secular spirit—the idea of man as a completely reasonable being but by no means a person divinely appointed to rule the universe—was widespread. Secular philosophy held an almost equal importance with Christianity, while the simple devotion to God which we find in so much verse of the seventeenth century often became lost in banal hymns and prayers.

What brought about this change? Can we put a date to it? The answer to the second question is a firm "No", but the answer to the first must be sought for carefully and with much study. Rose Macaulay, in *Religious Elements in Literature*, has some interesting things to say on this subject:

> Mysticism was out of fashion, the metaphysical school long gone, "wild divinity" no more, Sir Thomas Browne's "wingy mysteries" impaled on pins for inspection, Donne, Browne, Herbert, Vaughan, Crashaw, and Milton all gone into the world of light, leaving behind them a less starry generation, who gazed on the heavens through telescopes, and observed with awe and gratification the intelligence of

the Creator through the order of the universe. . . . The finest intelligences were not feeling mystically devout, but were otherwise, or agreed with Dr Johnson, that "poetic devotion cannot often please", though "the doctrines of religion may be defended in a didactic poem".

Here we come upon apologetics and didacticism regarded as a suitable subject for poetry. Poems are no longer written either purely in praise of God, or as personal overflows of private devotion. In this age they are to be used as argument; in other words—with a few exceptions—they are to take their place among the various modes for expressing philosophical ideas; it is almost as if Wittgenstein were to burst into song when he became possessed by some abstruse idea.

To us now, all this seems a rather ludicrous thing, but we have to remember that poetry in the eighteenth century was very much a public medium. Few subjects were thought unsuitable for it; Dr Johnson certainly spoke often of decorum in verse, but he was usually referring to form and artifice rather than to subject-matter or ideas. Yet this public nature of verse showed all the defects of its virtues; poets may have possessed patrons, there may have been many actual and potential readers of poetry, but the very virtues present in these things also meant that, unless one were a Dr Johnson (whose prose, anyway, was his real medium) or a Swift, one was liable quickly to slip into complacency and repetition. Poetry, and especially Christian poetry, implies and demands a struggle. Public verse in the distant past in England—I am thinking especially of the ballads—not only had a struggle with language itself but was at almost constant war with the need to be general and the urge to be personal and particular. And verse, in early times, though it may have had very strict conventions, depended very much on the nameless poets who brought in innovations and constantly exercised their own imaginations with new stories and images.

The eighteenth century, on the other hand, suffered from the great literary events of the previous hundred years. It was, I suppose, a period of consolidation; there was no need for experiment, and where there is no experiment, any art tends to become moribund.

On the whole, in this book, I have dealt with the poets in question in strictly chronological order; occasionally, I shall deviate from this, with, for example, Blake, who, though not an orthodox Christian at all, cannot be omitted from any study of English Christian poetry. For a number of reasons he fits more easily into the Romantic Period than into the eighteenth century, even though he started writing at the latter time.

Something must now be said about the dominant moral fervour of the eighteenth century—the urge to preach and teach, the desire to discuss good and evil rather than the love of God for man. In a sense, Christianity was brought down to human terms, to what man wanted and thought desirable, rather than to what God had planned for him. Let us look, for a moment, at a passage from Pope's *Essay on Man*:

> Know then thyself, presume not God to scan,
> The proper study of Mankind is Man.
> Plac'd on this isthmus of a middle state,
> A Being darkly wise and rudely great:
> With too much knowledge for the Sceptic side,
> With too much weakness for the Stoic's pride,
> He hangs between; in doubt to act or rest;
> In doubt to deem himself a God, or beast;
> In doubt his mind or body to prefer;
> Born but to die, and reas'ning but to err;

. . . .

Chaos of Thought and Passion, all confused;
Still by himself abused, or disabused;

. . . .

So be judge or Truth, in endless Error hurled:
The glory, jest, and riddle of the world!

This is a splendid piece of rhetoric, but it is more than merely that, I think. It has claims to poetry because of its precision, assurance and wit and language combined in a decorous and suitable form. Poets of the eighteenth century were passionately devoted to the heroic couplet, and there is no doubt that many of them overworked the medium; Pope, the greatest heroic couplet writer of them all, seldom becomes boring, mainly because he is witty and sensitive enough to see when a particular literary device is growing threadbare and wearisome. Even when he has little to say, he can say it either with mock grandeur or with apt wit.

A knowledge of what Pope himself thought about wit and taste—the twin gods of the eighteenth century—is well expressed by Edward Nibes Hooker in his essay, *Pope on Wit: The "Essay on Criticism"*:

In the first place, Pope at the start, after describing the highest form of artistic talent in the poet as true genius, and the highest gift of the critic as true taste, proceeds to the principle that the best critics are those who excel as authors. True taste, therefore, is best revealed in the operations of genius.... Or, since genius is distressingly rare, one may, like Pope, examine the ways of wit, that more inclusive thing, conceived of as literary talent or as the distinguishing element in literature, the breath informing the dull clay.

It must be remarked here that wit and taste are scarcely major virtues; they have nothing to do with the Seven Gifts of the Holy Ghost. One wonders, then, did Pope, a Catholic, deliberately keep apart his poetry and his religion?

Or did he honestly give an importance to a quality like taste which we today, who are also Christians, find it very difficult to comprehend? Firstly, I think we must bear in mind the fact that to a poet of the eighteenth century qualities like grace, elegance, wit and taste were an essential part of the general concept then of man's fall from grace and of the Redemption. Once we realize this, we can see that what to us appears trivial or inessential was to men like Dr Johnson and Pope something of religious significance. What appears, then, at first sight, to be a dislocation between two things is really an attempt at, and usually a realization of, unity.

There were, of course, as in every age, the victims of the eighteenth-century attitude—writers like Cowper and Smart, who were searching their innermost beings for the truth about themselves and the meaning of life. Such men often had what we would now call nervous breakdowns. Even Dr Johnson himself was a victim of a terrible melancholia which today would probably be called "depression" and might well be relieved by drugs or electric shock treatment. But perhaps Christopher Smart and William Cowper are the most touching and talented examples of poets whom the spirit of the age drew into madness. Smart was able to exact from his suffering a powerful mystical poetry, as we can see in the following stanzas from his *A Song to David*:

> For Adoration, in the dome
> Of Christ, the sparrows find a home,
>   And on his olives perch:
> The swallows also dwell with thee,
> O man of God's humility,
>   Within his Saviour's Church.
>
>   . . . .

Sweet the young nurse, with love intense,
Which smiles o'er sleeping innocence;
    Sweet, when the lost arrive:
Sweet the musician's ardour beats,
While his vague mind's in quest of sweets,
    The choicest flowers to hive.

. . . .

Glorious—more glorious—is the crown
Of Him that brought salvation down,
    By meekness call'd thy Son:
Thou that stupendous truth believed;—
And now the matchless deed's achieved,
    DETERMINED, DARED, and DONE!

This is a poem of joy and celebration. Cowper, whose biography, *The Stricken Deer*, was so finely and understandingly written by Lord David Cecil, was haunted all his adult life by the obsession that he was not among the saved. His poems, unhappily, try to avoid too overt an approach to this subject, yet hints of the man's misery and sickness do appear now and again:

I hate the sins that made thee mourn
And drove thee from my breast.
                (*Walking with God*)
Lord, it is my chief complaint,
That my love is weak and faint.
                (*Lovest Thou Me?*)
Oh happy peasant! Oh unhappy bard!

. . . .

He lost in errors his vain heart prefers,
She safe in the simplicity of hers.
                (*Simple Faith*)

This sad but unself-pitying poetry, which transcends the simple hymn forms that it uses, is absolutely honest and direct and, in its way, marks the real beginning of the expression of self-consciousness, together with the romanticized longing for the natural life of the soil, which was to reach its apotheosis in *The Lyrical Ballads*. Perhaps also it reaches back to Langland's *Vision*, though no two ways of actually writing poetry could be more different.

But we are moving away from the main subject of this chapter, namely, the attitude towards Christianity and its expression in verse in the eighteenth century. This age has so often been called the Age of Reason; but even in the brief survey we have so far made of it we can see clearly that beneath the clarity, order and smoothness a good deal of turmoil was going on. This turmoil was to be expressed most honestly in the Romantic age, and with absolute freedom in our own time.

Some of the greatest writers of the eighteenth century, or Augustan age, as it has also been called, were prose writers. In his fascinating collection of philosophical passages taken from work by eighteenth-century philosophers, Isaiah Berlin compares the ideas of Locke, Berkeley, Hume and others; he declares:

> Berkeley, so far from finding this empiricism unpalatable because he is a Christian and a bishop, on the contrary finds it alone compatible with the spiritualism which impregnates all his beliefs. For him Locke is, if anything, not empiricist enough. And, in a sense, Berkeley is right ... Berkeley quite consistently rejects attempts at "appeasement" of physics, and rejects all efforts at compromise with its alleged demands.... For Berkeley the notion of external substances so cut off from possible sensible experience (like Aquinas, oddly perhaps, Locke on the one hand believed that all human knowledge came through the senses) ... is unintelligible.

In other words, for Berkeley "the senses are the sole source of knowledge. The world consists of thoughts, feelings, sensations—'ideas' in the minds of agents, of God, and his creatures, men." It is easy to see how inept was Dr Johnson's foolish answer to Berkeley when he kicked a stone and said, "Sir, thus I refute you." He was displaying lack of understanding not only of Berkeley's views but of all philosophy since Plato and Aristotle.

So far, it would seem that I have done little else but demonstrate the reasonableness of eighteenth-century philosophy. In fact, my intention is not only to show the very different philosophical, metaphysical and religious views displayed by the best thinkers of the time but also to make clear how these differences were undoubtedly paving the way for the agnosticism of some of the nineteenth-century poets. Darwinism, of course, had much to do with the later agnosticism and rejection of Christianity, but a deep faith would not be so easily overthrown had the beginnings of doubt not been suggested, however remotely, in the previous century.

We have seen already how the presiding spirit of Augustan Christianity was a taste for morality and for discourse on moral views, rather than for either an interest in dogma or a desire for visionary experience. It may be that the last-named of these experiences had received a full expression in the seventeenth century; perhaps men of religion in the eighteenth century reacted strongly against the very suggestion of a transcendental God. One feels indeed, at times, that the God of this age was merely a rather frightening superhuman spirit whom it was unwise to approach too nearly or too intimately. The common man believed in his presence, yes, but I rather doubt if this particular divinity was a God of compassion and mercy. Maybe he was nearer the Jewish Yahweh than Jesus Christ.

Such speculations are not always valuable, however. The main difficulties which the eighteenth century presents are the numerous religious beliefs and secular philosophies, together with a most definite godless and materialistic spirit, which were found along with the development of a rich middle class. In this, the century seems very close to our own, though at least at that time culture was not derided nor poets secretly scoffed at. We have seen already how such a reliance on material things often brought madness in its wake; we know that bedlam existed, that people were thrown into cold water as a kind of early form of shock treatment; but we also know that it was possible for a poet like Gray to write the following lines and not be accused of escapism:

> Perhaps in this neglected spot is laid
>   Some heart once pregnant with celestial fire;
> Hands, that the rod of empire might have sway'd,
>   Or waked to ecstasy the living lyre.

> But Knowledge to their eyes her ample page
>   Rich with the spoils of time did ne'er unroll;
> Chill Penury repress'd their noble rage,
>   And froze the genial current of the soul.
>   (*Elegy written in a Country Churchyard*)

This marble-like repose seems, at times, to belong to another world than ours; yet it has a classical beauty, a deep sincerity that make up for what may seem to us chilly and distant at the same time.

The satirical, often bitter Swift, on the other hand, kept little from his readers; he vented his spleen both in his prose and verse. He could be tender, certainly, but his best-known mood is anger and mockery:

> The Vermin only tease and pinch
> Their Foes superior by an inch
>
>   . . . .

Thus every Poet in his Kind
Is bit by him that comes behind;
Who, though too little to be seen,
Can tease, and gall, and give the Spleen.

(Critics)

But Swift, much as he suffered in various ways, could laugh at himself too; in his *Verses on the Death of Dr Swift*, he wrote:

Behold the fatal day arrive!
"How is the Dean?"—"He's not alive."
Now the departing prayer is read:
"He hardly reads"—"The Dean is dead."

. . . .

He's dead, you say; then let him rot;
I'm glad the medals were forgot.

The eighteenth century and the Christianity manifested in it do indeed seem complex when we compare them with the previous age. With the exception of the nineteenth and twentieth centuries, the eighteenth is, without doubt, by far the most difficult to deal with from the Christian point of view. Morality had become more important than dogma or any kind of didacticism; yet, on the other hand, most of the poets of the period admitted and paid homage to a Divinity which was transcendent rather than immanent. Mystical experience as an awareness of God in a particularly close and intimate way was, as we say now, "out". I suppose the most general way in which the Christian God was regarded was as Pope saw him, that is to say, as:

But all mankind's concern is Charity;
All must be false that thwart this One great End;
And all of God, that bless Mankind, or men.

(Essay on Man)

Three centuries—the seventeenth, eighteenth and nineteenth—these could scarcely be more different in their attitude to Christianity. All that they shared, probably, was a general belief in Christian morality and a lack (at least at the end of each century) of a fierce didacticism. What the seventeenth- and some of the nineteenth-century poets did have in common, however, was a desire for mystical union with God. We must not forget that, although he was discovered so much later, Gerard Manley Hopkins was in fact a Victorian poet. So were Francis Thompson and Coventry Patmore. These poets shared with Donne, Vaughan, Herbert, Crashaw and Traherne a desire to find God in some kind of transcendental way. But it was doubt, I think, that was the chief religious characteristic of some of the nineteenth-century poets; they suffered deeply from "philosophical anxiety", as a young, now dead, Greek poet aptly put it. But these Romantic and Victorian poets demand a chapter of their own and do not fit into one which contains a consideration of the Augustan attitude to Christianity.

CHAPTER VII

THE NINETEENTH
CENTURY

The nineteenth century was, paradoxically, rich in material prosperity (for some) and in the variety of poets and poetry it produced. One recalls that Coleridge and Wordsworth had written their *Preface to Lyrical Ballads*, with its introduction about the necessity of poetry being written in the language "of ordinary men", at the beginning of the period with which this chapter deals; while at the end, we find the often florid verse of Dowson, Wilde and Lionel Johnson. In between are the great ones, the real Victorians (I am not, of course, denying greatness to other Romantic poets) —Keats, Shelley, Byron, Browning and Tennyson. What have these men to do with Christianity? Did any or all of them adhere to it completely? What effect did it have on their work?

These are large questions and maybe one can only answer them by studying in detail the individual attitude towards religion which each of these poets manifested. As an undergraduate, Shelley declared himself to be an atheist, but, judging from his later work, one can see that, in the literal sense, he was nothing of the sort. He was a kind of mystic whom Professor Zaehner, in *Mysticism: Sacred and Profane*, has defined as the sort of man who wants to lose himself completely in natural objects. Thus, when Shelley writes, in *Ode to the West Wind*:

> Make me thy lyre, even as the forest is:
>   What if my leaves are falling like its own?
> The tumult of thy mighty harmonies
>   Will take from both a deep autumnal tone,
> Sweet though in sadness. Be thou, Spirit fierce,
>   My spirit! Be thou me, impetuous one!

Shelley's rapturous songs are not in the least escapist; his own spirit and character were, in many ways, as ethereal as those of the natural objects in which he took such delight.

But to write at all of the Romantic poets, when we are making a survey of the greatest poets of the nineteenth century, seems somehow to give an unreal picture of the Victorian age. So much that we regard as typically Victorian—its furniture, huge meals, lengthy novels, political change and social dissatisfaction—seems far more than a decade or two removed from the Romantic Movement. This is not wholly illusion. The Romantics really did mark a quite separate, though fairly brief literary movement of their own; such movements have occasionally arisen in English literature, but there certainly does seem to be something especially startling about the differences between most eighteenth-century poets, Romantics, and nineteenth-century poets. Is it that we see the differences enlarged or inflated simply because we observe them now from the distance of over a hundred years? No, I think the whole question is subtler and more complex than this. And it is essential that we remember that there were many things which the Romantics and the Victorian poets shared—a love of form, for instance, a taste for myth, a delight in pure song and lyricism. But in one most important matter, they did differ; like the poets of the eighteenth century, those of the nineteenth had a firm conviction that poetry could, or even ought, to be a vehicle for moral opinion. I am not now thinking of Browning's rather trite

> God's in His heaven—
> All's right with the world!

Recently critics and readers have (I think, mistakenly) cited these lines as the typical thoughts of a rather simple mind. In fact, Browning was a highly complex thinker, as we can see in the poem *Any Wife to Any Husband*:

> Pride?—when those eyes forestal the life behind
> The death I have to go through I—when I find
> > Now that I want thy help most, all of thee!.
> What did I fear? Thy love shall hold me fast
> Until the little minute's sleep is past
> > And I wake saved—And yet it will not be!

Browning's dramatic manner, his occasional flights into melodrama, and, above all, his live, rich goodness of feeling —all these things make it impossible for us to regard him as anything but a genuine, though often unorthodox, Christian. His wife's lush and rhetorical *Sonnets from the Portuguese* seem very mediocre by comparison.

Difficult as a poet, Browning was very straightforward as a man. He spent a large part of his life nursing a wife whose sickness was, to a great extent, hypochondriac; there is no record that he ever grew impatient with or envied her the reputation which was so much greater than his own. Time has redressed the balance and her well-meaning love *Sonnets from the Portuguese*, with their phrases such as "How do I love thee?" have become very dated. Like Rupert Brooke later, emotion and sensibility were more important than what one made of them. Robert Browning, on the other hand, though he may have been guilty at times of a glib optimism, was not only a real thinker in verse, which is by no means the same thing as a prose philosopher, but a dramatic poet, who could write monologues such as *Soliloquy in a Spanish Cloister*, *Andrea del Sarto*, *Fra Lippo Lippi*, as well as beautifully controlled love lyrics like *Parting at Morning*, *Life in a Love*, and *Two in the Campagna*. His care of and love for his wife seems to have bought out the essential virility in him; perhaps the conflict it may have set up was the spring from which his best verse flowered.

I have deliberately spoken of Browning before I deal with Keats. No men could have been more different, yet each shared courage, a love of language, a dramatic sense and the need for human passion. In respect of the last, both were thwarted, though in quite different ways.

But what has all this to do with Christianity? Browning was more orthodox than Keats (who was always an empirical thinker), but, as I have said in an earlier chapter, a man's actions are motivated by his beliefs. Both poets endured a good deal of mental and/or physical suffering (in the case of Browning, it was completely mental), but both avoided self-pity. One is reminded of Lawrence Durrell's fine line,

The suffering **hidden** under gentleness.

Browning, in his own day, was attacked for his obscurity, and there is a pleasant story that, one day, when asked by an earnest woman the meaning of a particular poem, he declared, "Madam, when I wrote that line two people knew what it meant, God and Robert Browning; now only God knows."

Keats suffered from the obtuseness of critics who hated what was new and exciting. Many readers, indeed, have thought that the shock of some of the reviews hastened his death by consumption; I suppose it may well have done so, and yet one feels that he was too courageous a writer to be so affected. On the other hand, the accumulation of per-

sonal sickness, illness in the family and the knowledge that
he was unlikely ever to realize his great and undoubtedly
ambitious poetic plans affected him profoundly. It is amazing to consider just how much he did write when one
remembers that he died at the age of twenty-six.

In his *Letters*, where Keats refers to "the Holiness of the
Heart's affections and the truth of Imagination", he makes
a statement as close to anything Christian which could
possibly be envisaged. Yet, in truth, Keats' religion was a
Platonic worship of beauty; if we wish to equate beauty
with God, then he was a Theist, if not a Christian. It would
be foolish to try to prove and strain similarities, but there
are certainly sufficient Christian attitudes to make it worth-
while to consider Keats in this book. Christianity, after all,
does not possess *all* the virtues, or all the subtle philosophical notions either. In the latter case, it has itself
acknowledged its debt to Aristotle in the person of Thomas
Aquinas, the Church's accepted and greatest thinker.

When we come to the verse of Coleridge, we discover a
much more portentous thinker in prose (even if he did, in
the *Biographia Literaria*, sum up, with great lucidity, the
difference between the Primary and Secondary Imagination);
there is little of the lightness or wit which is constantly
springing out of Keats' *Letters*. On the other hand, both
poets had a taste for myth, fantasy, or the macabre.
Christabel by Coleridge may interestingly be compared
with Keats' *Lamia* or *St Agnes' Eve*. Keats, however, wrote
nothing to be compared with *The Ancient Mariner* or
Kubla Khan. One does not easily forget the following
stanzas from *The Ancient Mariner* (the sense of guilt re-
solved is wonderfully conveyed):

> O sleep! it is a gentle thing,
> Beloved from pole to pole!
> To Mary Queen the praise be given!
> She sent the gentle sleep from Heaven!,
> That slid into my soul.

Or the following lines, taken from *Frost At Midnight* (Coleridge is watching his child, who is sleeping):

> Dear Babe, that sleepest cradled by my side,
> Whose gentle breathings, heard in this deep calm
> Fill up the interspersed vacancies
> And momentary pauses of the thought!
> ...... I was reared
> In the great city, pent mid cloisters dim,
> And saw nought lovely but the sun and stars.
> But *thou*, my babe! shalt wander like a breeze
> By lakes and sandy shores, beneath the crags
> Of ancient mountain, and beneath the clouds,
> Which image in their bulk both lakes and shores
> And mountain crags: so shalt thou see and hear
> The lovely shapes and sounds intelligible
> Of that eternal language, which my God
> Utters, who from eternity doth teach
> Himself in all, and all things in himself.
> Great universal Teacher! He shall mould
> Thy spirit, and by giving make it ask.

This is very reminiscent of Wordsworth, though while it contains a definite mystical content, that content is Christian, not pantheist (for example, "Himself in all, and all things in himself ... Great universal Teacher!", and so on).

Tennyson, on the other hand, was one of the great doubters of the century, and it must be admitted that at times he did make rather "a song and dance about it". His *In Memoriam*, though, is for the most part, a noble and majestic poem, but it certainly has its moments of banality, which arise, I think, from the poet's ill-developed sense of humour:

> O joy to him in this retreat,
> I wanted in ambrosial dark
> To drink the cooler air and mark
> The landscape wintering thro' the heat.

O sound to rout the brood of cares,
    The sweep of sound in morning dew,
    The gust that round the garden flew
And tumbled half the mellowing pears!

Though capable of great depths of feeling, Tennyson had very little to say. He also had, as Auden has pointed out, a flawless ear; but an unusual sense of music is no compensation for the lack of interesting subject-matter. His religious doubt was his main material; for the rest, he went on at great length, simply with a gift for music and a powerful visual imagination. One tends to prefer the occasional roughness of Browning, who always had a very great deal to say, and a more exciting, original way in which to say it, than the bland numbers of Tennyson.

Wordsworth, the other great long-liver of the nineteenth century, wrote, if anything, even more prolificly than Tennyson; but whereas Tennyson had no constant obsession or subject, Wordsworth, throughout his life, was attempting to express a form of pantheism, a search which ended, however, in orthodox Christian belief. But it must be admitted that the poems which appeared in his last years have nothing of the dignity, detail or beauty which those of the early and middle periods manifest, and possess very little interest. Wordsworth was not, like Keats, a man who really found himself poetically as a man.

With Coleridge, in the late 1790's, he collaborated in producing *The Lyrical Ballads*, a literary manifesto of great importance. It contained poems by both editors and was a powerful reaction against the artificial poetic diction of the earlier eighteenth century. Both poets sought a simple, direct poetic speech, "the language of ordinary men", and both tended to take a rather Romantic view of rural life. Of the two poets, Coleridge was the more truly orthodox. Wordsworth's earlier poems tended to show that pantheism which searched for union with God, but which sought not a personal God so much as a divinity which was by and filled everything, both the natural world and the heart of man. I suppose *The Prelude* is the best example of this searching, yet I am inclined to think that *Lines Composed a Few Miles Above Tintern Abbey* conveys more succinctly the poet's true beliefs and aspirations. It contains passages which express precisely Wordsworth's type of religion:

> ...... Nor less, I trust,
> To whom I may have owed another gift,
> Of aspect more sublime; that blessed mood,
> In which the burthen of the mystery,
> In which the heavy and the weary weight
> Of all this unintelligible world,
> Is lightened:—that serene and blessed mood,
>
> .   .   .   .
>
> While with an eye made quiet by the power
> Of harmony, and the deep power of joy,
> We see into the life of things.

This may not express the Christianity with which we are all familiar—indeed, many would say that the experiences it describes are not Christian at all. Yet no one could deny that Wordsworth was in search of the truth about nature and reality. In his *Ode: Intimations of Immortality*, he declares:

> Hence in a season of calm weather
> Though inland far we be,
> Our souls have sight of that immortal sea
> Which brought us hither,
> Can in a moment travel thither,
> And see the children sport upon the shore,
> And hear the mighty waters rolling evermore.

Here Wordsworth uses much of the language of Christian orthodoxy—"soul", "immortal", and so on; and in other passages of the ode he uses even more of them. What was his purpose in writing this poem? How far were his religious sympathies drawn to Christianity? It is not easy to answer all these questions, but it *is* easy to see that Wordsworth, though he was not a deeply original thinker, felt with his emotions. There is nothing wrong about this activity, so long as the poet does not mistake feeling for thought. Wordsworth had a very different kind of mind from that of Coleridge. Coleridge was deeply reflective, fundamentally philosophical. In a number of ways, in fact, Wordsworth scarcely fits into this study. His late ecclesiastical poems are heavy, contrived, far from his best work.

The flamboyant, prolific, rich flow of Byron's verse seems hardly to find a place in a book about Christian poetry. Yet, in spite of all the rhetoric and histrionic attitudes in his poetry, and the scandals in his life, of which he was almost equally proud, he had also a conventionality and a childish desire to shock (which is perhaps only the reverse side of wishing to be conventional)—in spite of all these things Byron had a vein (hard to find sometimes, it is true) of genuine faith and of a desire for God in his poetry. It is this orthodox Christian vein that has made me want to say something about him in this study. It is when he is being most straightforward and honest that Byron shows this tender and humble attitude towards religion:

> They were alone once more; for them to be
>   Thus was another Eden; they were never
> Weary, unless when separate: the tree
>   Cut from its forest root of years—the river
> Damm'd from its fountain—the child from the knee
>   And breast maternal wean'd at once for ever—
> Would wither less than these two torn apart;.
> Alas! there is no instinct like the heart—

When Byron writes rather dramatically of his desire for the life of a hermit in the desert he is completely unconvincing—the idea is, anyway, grotesque for a man such as he—but when he discourses of the love of God and men, he is deeply moving.

Matthew Arnold is a very different case altogether. In some ways he is the typical Victorian, the son of an overbearing father, and himself a thinker and doubter. Like so many intellectuals of his age, he suffered deeply from religious difficulties; the physical world seemed to have expanded, and scientists were drawing conclusions that appeared to be at odds with revealed religion. Arnold expressed the feelings which were common among thoughtful men. A fine poem, and also a specially good example of this particularly Victorian viewpoint, is *To Marguerite*:

> Yes: in the sea of life enisled,
>   With echoing straits between us thrown.
> Dotting the shoreless watery wild,
>   We mortal millions live *alone*.
> The islands feel the enclasping flow,
> And then their endless bounds they know.
>
> . . . .
>
> Who order'd that their longing's fire
>   Should be, as soon as kindled, cool'd?
> Who renders vain their deep desire?—
>   A God, a God their severance ruled;
> And bade betwixt their shores to be
> The unplumb'd, salt, estranging sea.

This poem expresses the general Romantic Victorian mood. Indeed, I have included examinations of poets like Arnold, Byron and Keats, who, in the most rigid sense, cannot really be called Christians, because they express a yearning for Christianity which bears such a close resemblance to the creed itself that it would be a falsification of the spirit of the whole century not to mention it at least.

When we come to Catholics like Newman, Patmore, Wilde (converted at the very end of his life), Francis

Thompson and, above all, Hopkins (whose work was not published until this century), we are in genuine difficulties. For the fact is that, with the exception of Hopkins, most of them are very minor indeed. Lionel Johnson and Dowson —what can be said of them when Browning, Byron and Keats are considered? Only that, however fervent a man's religion may be, it does not necessarily make him a good poet. But this subject is examined more fully in the final chapter.

It may be that *because* they were writing against the spirit and general philosophical tendencies of the age these men often seem lukewarm. All the agony of mind that has already gone into the writing of *The Hound of Heaven* does not make this poem seem like a real battle between God and man; when we think of Herbert or Vaughan, we feel how feeble Thompson's verse is, however honest his intentions. His best poem seems to me to be *The Kingdom of God*:

> O World invisible, we view thee,
> O world intangible, we touch thee,
> O world unknowable, we know thee,
> Inapprehensible, we clutch thee!
>
> Does the fish soar to find the ocean,
> The eagle plunge to find the air—
> That we ask of the stars in motion
> If they have rumour of thee there?
>
> . . . .
>
> Yea, in the night, my Soul, my daughter,
> Cry,—clinging Heaven by the hems;
> And lo, Christ walking on the water,
> Not of Gennesareth, but Thames!

These lines have a depth and simplicity which *The Hound of Heaven* lacks. The latter poem is too histrionic, too demanding of *our* acquiescence, to make the effect the poet is really after. But, as later with Chesterton or Belloc, Catholics have tended to stress the purple patches in poets of their own persuasion when the quietness of a piece like *The Kingdom of God* has a beautiful candour and simplicity which are often overlooked.

Newman, of course, is always hauled up as the finest, if not the greatest, Catholic poet of the nineteenth century. But his fame really rests on his *Apologia Pro Vita Sua*, not on his poems or hymns at all. None the less, *The Pillar of the Cloud* is worth quoting from; in it, Newman seems to be expressing the metaphysical gloom which so often troubled a Catholic and a convert at this time:

> So long thy power hath blest me, sure it still
> > Will lead me on,
> O'er moor and fen, o'er crag and torrent, till
> > The night is gone;
> And with the morn those angel faces smile
> Which I have loved long since and lost a while.

Though the two final lines of this poem quite literally make one shudder, the rest does convey the sadness and disappointment of Newman's life.

The Catholic poets of the nineties are very slight indeed. Wilde's *Ballad of Reading Gaol* (one of the best things he ever wrote) contains one memorable stanza, but little else that is moving or original:

> Yet each man kills the things he loves,
> > By each let this be heard,
> Some do it with a bitter look,
> > Some with a flattering word,
> The coward does it with a kiss,
> > The brave man with a sword.

Obviously, the chief temptation of Catholics is to blow up the reputations of writers like Thompson, Alice Meynell,

Dowson and Lionel Johnson whose talents are really of small stature. Coventry Patmore, the poet of occasionally embarrassing poems in praise of married love, could also produce the following vivid piece of descriptive writing:

> Here, in this little Bay,
> Full of tumultous life and great repose,
> Where, twice a day,
> The purposeless, glad ocean comes and goes,
> Under high cliffs, and far from the huge town,
> I sit me down.
> For want of me the world's course will not fail:
> When all its work is done, the lie shall rot;
> The truth is great, and shall prevail,
> When none cares whether it prevail or not.
>
> (*Magna Est Veritas*)

There are two important women visionary poets who, in some ways, are the most interesting of the religious poets of the nineteenth century—Emily Brontë and Emily Dickinson. Both are poets who write formal poems which express strange experiences of an unmistakably mystical nature. Of the two poets, Emily Dickinson, an American, was far the most prolific. Neither woman seems to be precisely an orthodox Christian, but Emily Brontë does seem closer to conventional Christianity, even though she also dwells in a world, not exactly of fantasy, but certainly one that is some lonely, lofty, private place:

> What I love shall come like visitant of air,
> Safe in secret power from lurking human snare;
> What loves me, no word of mine shall e'er betray,
> Though for faith unstained my life must forfeit pay.
>
> (from *The Visionary*)

Emily Brontë is a visionary of the Wordsworthian kind, a seeker after union with Nature and a kind of divinity who is pantheistic rather than personal. She also experiences intimations of future and present joy:

> How beautiful the Earth is still
> To thee—how full of Happiness;
> How little fraught with real ill,
> Or shadowy phantoms of distress.
>
> > (from *Anticipation*)

And in *The Visionary*, she describes, with wonderful economy, exactly what her particular kind of mystical awareness feels like:

> Silent is the house; all are laid asleep:
> One alone looks out o'er the snow-wreaths deep,
> Watching every cloud, dreading every breeze
> That whirls the wildering drift, and bends the
> > groaning trees.

Emily Dickinson's verse is even more visionary than that of Emily Brontë; but it is also always firmly attached to concrete things, so that her strange, metaphysical experiences are conveyed to her readers with a reality and conviction that must have been very hard to attain. None of her poems are given titles, so that it would seem that she wishes to leave her readers to make what they can of her verse, to enter her world or leave it alone; she does not seem to care much which they do, since she is one of those poets who *must* express themselves, whether anyone reads them or not. As James Reeves has said of her:

> Friends were her estate, but language was her province, and she delighted in it, whether in verse or in prose. She had what can only be called an aristocratic spirit, high-minded

but without a trace of priggishness, serious without self-importance, shrewd enough to be malicious had she wished, but too gentle and kind for malice.... Her universe was bounded by infinite horizons, presided over by dawns, sunsets and mountains, clothed with trees and flowers, inhabited by birds, beasts and insects; yet it was not the Romantic world of pantheistic nature in which man was an intruder. ... Heaven and earth were co-extensive, and Emily believed fervently in both. Her Eternity is an eternity of space rather than of time.

We can see what Reeves means by these remarks if we quote the whole of one remarkable poem, No. 44:

> The soul selects her own society,
> Then shuts the door.
> To her divine majority
> Present no more.
>
> Unmoved she notes the chariots pausing
> At her low gate;
> Unmoved, an Emperor be kneeling
> Upon her mat.
>
> I've known her from an ample nation
> Choose one,
> Then close the valves of her attention
> Like stone.

It is easy to see that this is very original religious verse. Can it, in fact, be called Christian at all, when the poet seems not to have been in search of a personal God, but rather concerned with completing and understanding her own private world? To make this latter remark is, I believe, an illusion; because Emily seldom mentions God or Christ by name, this does not mean that she was indifferent to him. To praise God's world and to want to repeat it in words is a humble Christian act. It is also an act of great charity.

But of course the great late Victorian poet, though it seems almost ludicrous to call him "Victorian", is Gerard Manley Hopkins. Withheld from publication until this century by Robert Bridges' wrong-headed decision. Hopkins does, nevertheless, come within the Victorian period and so must be included in a chapter on nineteenth-century Christian literature. Along with the surprising discovery of Traherne in this century, Hopkins is undoubtedly the anomaly of his, and our, age. A celibate, a Jesuit, a sensuous poet, an amazing poetic experimentalist who invented new rhythms and forms (these were largely what alarmed Bridges), a lonely priest who wrote some of the best poems that had been written for fifty years—he is a problem indeed.

I think the best study of Hopkins is still Leavis' in *New Bearings in English Poetry*; this is an essay of remarkable sensitivity, far ahead of its time, and showing a rare identification and understanding of critic with poet. Apart from Hopkins' own letters and notebooks, it is the most valuable piece of writing that we have on Hopkins.

What is unique in this poet is his dynamic sense of God, as we can see in *The Windhover*:

> I caught this morning morning's minion, king-
> dom of daylight's dauphin, dapple-dawn-
> drawn Falcon in his riding
> Of the rolling level underneath him steady
> air, and striding
>
> High. . . .

But Hopkins' intensity could often, and was often, tempered by his gentleness and love of natural objects and, especially, by innocence:

> O surely, reaving Peace, my Lord should leave in lieu
> Some good . . . . . . he does leave Patience exquisite,
> That plumes to peace hereafter . . . .
>
> (from *Peace*)

Ah Nature, framed in fault,
There's comfort, then, there's salt;
Nature, bad, base, and blind,
Dearly thou canst be kind;
There dearly then, dearly,
I'll cry thou canst be kind.

(from *Brothers*)

This poet made much of his invented words "inscape" and "instress"; the former meant the individuality of every living thing, while the latter meant both its being and intensity, and also our awareness of these things. Hopkins is regarded by almost everybody as a modern poet. He has had a strong influence on every twentieth-century poet from Auden downwards. He leads us, then, easily, into the Christian and near-Christian poets of our own age.

CHAPTER VIII

THE TWENTIETH CENTURY

This is an age of computers, wars, advertising and dislocated art. There are no longer any set laws which we can apply to art, no fixed rules at all in fact. And yet this is, perhaps, one of the most exciting ages in which to be an artist that most of us have ever known. We have Eliot, Auden, Muir and David Jones, it is true, but the last of these was, and is, the very reverse of conformist to this age; he has tried to weld typography, painting and poetry together, and in his *Anathemata* has for the most part succeeded. Eliot and Auden will be dealt with later in this chapter—just enough, I believe, since they came fairly late to Christianity and most of their early work has little or no place in this book.

What is unique about this age is the fact that the really Christian poets have had to be rebels. Christian culture has always continued, in however quiet a way, but the twentieth century has been more interested in Marxism, existentialism and Communism than in any other philosophy. And we have to remember that all poetry, however unconsciously, is created against a background of philosophy. Yet to be a rebel can also be creative, and perhaps some of the most interesting poets of this half-century have been those who have reacted, fiercely and strongly, against the *Zeitgeist*, or spirit of the age. Poetry never, when it is healthy, works in isolation. It always reacts to what is going on around it. To be powerful or great, it must be either rebellious or quietly existing in a world of its own. And this is by no means to be negative or escapist. We only have to examine some of the Christian poets of the present age to be quite sure of this.

Christians, and more especially Catholics, have tended to exalt writers such as Chesterton and Belloc into positions which are quite beyond their gifts or capacity. Both were minor poets of limited range, and to say this is not in any way to denigrate them. Good light verse demands severe disciplines—formal skill, a good ear, a wide vocabulary and a large range of poetic forms and language. Indeed, in some ways, light verse makes greater demands than serious. By this paradoxical remark, I mean that humorous, witty verse at ease with itself—though this is a statement which must obviously be immediately qualified—is in one sense, at least, harder to write than poetry which arises from the whole personality. For light, or semi-serious, verse relies almost completely on form and wit; if these things fail, then the writing in question fails almost completely. With serious poetry, on the other hand, a poet may be lacking in many skills which would seem to be essential to the making of poems, and yet produce a good, even a great poem.

Why is this? What is the reason for this apparent contradiction? The reason for it is mainly, I believe, that originality, novelty of subject, seriousness of purpose and intensity of feeling are more important than all skill and contrivance. This would seem to be an obvious enough point to make, but it is not clear to many Christian readers of verse, who are satisfied as long as the subject chosen is laudable and the treatment orthodox. The reason why Hopkins is so much greater than Francis Thompson and Newman is surely only explicable in these terms?

Yet one cannot write a study of Christian verse without

some reference to Belloc and Chesterton. Both have, it must be generally admitted, written better in prose than in poetry (one remembers especially Belloc's *Path to Rome* and Chesterton's wonderfully compressed *Thomas Aquinas*). But the verse of each seldom reaches the heights of true poetry, or transcends the limitations which both versifiers seem to feel obliged to impose upon it. Chesterton's best, and perhaps only, religious poem is *The Donkey*, which ends:

> Fools! For I also had my hour;
>   One far fierce hour and sweet:
> There was a shout about my ears,
>   And palms before my feet.

Belloc, a sadder, more melancholy man, seems to have been unable to express his dark moods in verse. The result is that only his hearty facetious side comes out in his poems; some of the worst characteristics of the Georgians —the smugness, the smallness, the refusal to be too experimental—manifest themselves in his verse, as, for example, in the conclusion of *The South Country*:

> If I ever become a rich man,
>   Or if ever I grow to be old,
> I will build a house with deep thatch
>   To shelter me from the cold,
> And there shall the Sussex songs be sung
>   And the story of Sussex told.
>
> I will hold my house in the high wood
>   Within a walk of the sea,
> And the men that were boys when I was a boy
>   Shall sit and drink with me.

But to be labelled a "Catholic" or a "Christian" poet is a difficult and disturbing thing. In the first place, it would appear to demand so much from the poet, to put so much pressure upon him. He tends to feel that his duty is first to his religion, whereas, at the risk of sounding blasphemous, I am prepared to say that the whole matter is the other way round. Once it is realized that all art—whatever its subject-matter or form—is a gift from God, there is no need to feel any conflict between the way in which Faith is expressed in verse forms, and the wholly secular art which is springing up now and which appears to be entirely alien to Christianity. A man or woman may write poems that are truly Christian without quite realizing it (Dylan Thomas, who wrote verse in praise of a God in whom, he said, he did not believe, is a good example). This is not an uncommon phenomenon, but it is not, alas, a subject with which I have much space to deal here. In general, I have only space for the fairly orthodox and the familiarly Christian.

But when we really begin to consider seriously the poets of the twentieth century, we find that the important or great Christian ones are not, as a rule, cradle Catholics; they are Anglicans, like T. S. Eliot, W. H. Auden, R. S. Thomas and Anne Ridler, or converts to Roman Catholicism, such as David Jones; or even Christians whom one can scarcely categorize (I am thinking now of David Gascoyne and Kathleen Raine). Of course, there are numerous minor Christian poets too—Ruth Pitter, for instance. And then there is the great controversial figure of Edith Sitwell, a poet whose greatest poem, *Still Falls the Rain*, is undoubtedly Christian in spirit and feeling, even though the poet herself did not enter the Church until some years later.

In many ways, the twentieth century is the hardest of all to deal with when one is writing of Christian poetry. In my final chapter, I hope to summarize the difficulties of the poet and critic in this age. In the meantime, it is only possible to say something in detail of what their Christianity adds to the work of a few selected poets, and also to consider the kind of difficulties which Christian poets in particular are confronted with in this age.

We must not, of course, forget that there *are* good Catholic poets writing now—the young writer Peter Levi, for example. In a sense, Peter Levi presents in person the very difficulties and conflict of which I have just been writing. He is not a poet who is *obviously* Christian; his battles and struggles with God are not carried out in new rhythms and rhyme-schemes, as Hopkins' were. A superficial reading of him would lead one to suppose that he is a compassionate nature poet, with a strong love of people and a great feeling for and understanding of classical Greece. His poems have a curious, carefree innocence—a quality one finds in no other contemporary poet, either Christian or non-Christian.

Edwin Muir tells us, in his *Autobiography*, that he had been a Christian all his life without "realizing it". A few critics are inclined to think that, just before his death, he moved into a kind of neo-Platonism, but certainly the poems of his last ten years or so are overtly Christian. Most of them are allegorical, and so they are not only interesting in themselves but also fascinating in the way that they demonstrate the subtleties and changes of mood that allegory can express. A beautiful example of this kind of work appears in his last book, *One Foot in Eden*. It is called simply *The Lord*, and ends:

> I would rather scour the roads a masterless dog,
> Than take such service, be a public fool,
> Obstreperous or tongue-tied, a good rogue,
> Than be with those, the clever and the dull,
> Who say that Lord is dead; when I can hear
> Daily his dying whisper in my ear.

In the twentieth century, the poet who comes closest to greatness is, of course, T. S. Eliot. His early, disillusioned poems, motivated by disgust with the modern world, have moved into the *Four Quartets*, one of the true mystical poems for perhaps over a century. In the *Quartets* (whose formal pattern is, incidentally, close to that of music), the poet reconciles the filth and evil of modern times—things perhaps over-emphasized in his early, non-Christian poems. Eliot was a convert to Anglo-Catholicism, and his Christianity, as manifested in *Four Quartets*, is, apart from much else, a poem of reconciliation; flesh and spirit are united in the Incarnation. As the poet writes in *Burnt Norton*, the first poem of the sequence:

> ......Other echoes
> Inhabit the garden. Shall we follow them
> Quick, said the bird, find them, find them,
> Round the corner......
> ......the roses
> Had the look of flowers that are looked at.
>
> . . . .
>
> And the lotos rose, quietly, quietly,
> The surface glittered out of heart of light...

The other three poems in the sequence, *East Coker*, *The Dry Salvages* and *Little Gidding*, are gradual steps towards a closer Christian union of God with man. In these long, beautifully melodious poems we find the struggle towards God re-enacted *within* the poetry; there is no feeling of a memory being recaptured or of a rare experience being transcribed.

In this chapter, Eliot should really be given the greatest amount of space; I am not writing about him at the length I should like, however, because I want to point out how, even in this un-Christian age, there are Christian poets who still write about their beliefs. They may not be working within a framework of orthodox Catholicism, but at least they are, in their very different ways, honouring or writing about the Christ of the Gospels.

R. S. Thomas is a Welsh Anglican parson and he has a dark vision of the world which embraces both man and nature. His poems are mainly concerned with the lives and troubles of his parishioners, the difficulties that the hard life of the soil brings to them. Christian compassion is the quality that is felt most strongly in his verse:

> He prayed for love, love that would share
> His rags' secret; rising he broke
> Like sun crumbling the gold air
>
> . . . .
>
> The live air for the starved folk.
>
> (*Bread*)

W. H. Auden is another poet who is a convert to Anglo-Catholicism. His poems, however, do not display that obsession with religion and mystical experience which we find in practically all Eliot's later work. Auden has one of those searching, probing minds which love esoteric items of knowledge for their own sake. That he has fastened on Anglicanism is not, though, a mere whim or hobby. His acceptance of Christianity is a matter of the mind as much as of the emotions, as indeed it should be; everything has, for him, to be tested by the intellect before it can be considered at all.

Auden never thrusts his Christianity at us. He has no wish either to convert or to speak much of his own conversion. Thus, in his lightest moods, he can write:

> Looking up at the stars I know quite well
> That, for all they care, I can go to hell,
> But on earth indifference is the least
> We have to dread from man or beast.
>
> . . . .

Were all stars to disappear or die,
I should learn to look at an empty sky
And feel its total dark sublime,
Though this might take me a little time.

(The More Loving One)

David Jones is the supreme example of the Christian artist. Both a painter and a poet, he draws on many traditions for his work—Welsh traditional stories and poetry, for instance, the liturgy of the Mass, and even his own experiences in the 1914 war, which he writes of at length in prose in *In Parenthesis*. There is no point in pretending that his fine poem, *Anathemata*, is not difficult; but it is not difficult for the same reasons that, for example, Pound's *Cantos* are. David Jones is not deliberately fragmentary—nor is he in any way influenced by the Imagist poets, as Pound was. He says, in the Introduction to *Anathemata*:

So it is that the present situation presents its own particular difficulties with regard to signs in general and the concept of sign. The whole complex of these difficulties is primarily felt by the sign-maker, the artist, because for him it is an immediate, day by day, factual problem. He has, somehow or other, to lift up valid signs; *that is his specific task* (italics mine). In practice, one of his main problems, one of the matters upon which his judgement is exercised ("The virtue of art is to judge") concerns the validity and availability of his images.

This makes fascinating reading, for it shows the twin virtues in Jones of a sense and use of tradition and a tremendous feeling for the present. He is doing, particularly in his poetry, something much more subtle than merely writing "Catholic poetry" in an age which is utterly alien to it; nor is he trying to recreate the mood of the Middle Ages (as William Morris and his followers did in the nineteenth century). No, what Jones is attempting is a dynamic poem in which the Office of the Church will be as lively and comprehensible as all that is going on in the world here and now. He is really in no sense a private or personal poet, but the magnitude of his task inevitably makes for difficulty, if not actual obscurity. But the best passages of *Anathemata* are clear and resonant:

<pre>
                on this hill
        at a time's turn
                not on any hill
        but on this hill
        (on this unabiding rock
                for one Great Summer
                        lifted up
                by next Great Winter
                        down
        among the altitudes
        with all help-heights
                        down
        as low as Parnassus.
</pre>

It would be idle to try to convince anyone that *Anathemata* is an easy poem, that the author's own profuse and helpful annotation is not essential, or that a good deal of hard work and learning are demanded from the reader. But, just as *The Waste Land* seemed utterly incomprehensible when it first appeared in 1922 but has now been absorbed into the general tradition of English poetry, so too, I believe, will the *Anathemata*, as poetry itself changes and develops, become more and more acceptable and assimilable. It is surely significant that the young poet and novelist, John Wain, is at present showing a great admiration for it.

Of the other Christian poets now writing—though often only fitfully—David Gascoyne is probably the most interesting. He started writing when very young and came much under the influence of Surrealist poets in Paris. Just before and during the 1939 war, however, his work changed completely. It showed a visionary quality of great power, and a feeling for Christ which can be compared with that of the greatest English mystical poets. Thus his *Miserere* (so reminiscent, in many ways, of Rouault's etchings on the same theme) ends:

> Not from a monstrance silver-wrought
> But from the tree of human pain
> Redeem our sterile misery
> Christ of Revolution and of Poetry,
> That man's long journey through the night
> May not have been in vain.

But perhaps Gascoyne's finest poem is his *The Gravel-Pit Field*; in this piece, one feels the very movement of the human mind and heart towards a close union with God:

> As with untold intensity
> On the far edge of Being, where
> Life's last faint forms begin to lose
> Name and identity and fade
> Away into the Void, endures
> The final thin triumphant flame
> Of all that's most despoiled and bare ...

From this necessarily brief survey of a few contemporary Christian poets, it would not seem that Christianity, whether it be Catholicism or not, is no longer a suitable subject for poetry, or that agnostic readers are totally uninterested in it. It is certainly true that a Christian poet today faces problems, both literary and doctrinal, which did not have to be considered or suffered in the time of Chaucer or of Spenser. But this is a matter which will be dealt with more fully in the final chapter. At the moment, we are still concerned, on the whole, with particular poets rather than with general questions.

CHAPTER IX

THE FOREIGNERS AND

MYSTICS

In a brief book such as this, I have found it necessary to restrict myself mainly to English poetry. To have attempted to cover Christian poetry from all over Europe would have been both ludicrous and useless. And yet to ignore completely such poets as Dante, Claudel, Péguy and Baudelaire would have created a terrible void. The reasons for my choice of the first three poets are surely obvious; Baudelaire I have included because, as T. S. Eliot pointed out, a man who trafficks with the devil knows more of God than one who is simply an agnostic or materialist. In other words, Baudelaire knew the spiritual world, even if only its dark side.

This chapter will also contain some general comments on the relations between poetry and Christian mysticism. This is a subject which has fascinated me for some time and, although I have already written about it at some length,[1] I feel that it is so central to Christian literature that a few comments on it are relevant here.

But to return to Christian poets who have written poetry in languages other than English—I propose to deal here with four of them—Baudelaire, Péguy, Claudel and Dante. The last, and greatest, will be treated at the end of this

[1] *Every Changing Shape*, London, Deutsch, 1961, and Chester Springs, Pa., Dufour Editions, 1962.

chapter. I have said already, Baudelaire has often been regarded as a *poète manqué*, as a man at odds with himself, a writer who fought out a personal conflict between God, the devil and himself. Through perversity, suffering, mockery and self-torture, Baudelaire retained a desire for God, even, one might say, a thirst for him. He admitted, for example, that "poetry is that which is the most real, that which is entirely true only in another world". Like Hopkins, Baudelaire questioned everything: unlike Hopkins, he was too caught up in the complexities of his own difficulties and doubts ever to approach God simply and humbly. But he is not to be reproached for this attitude. It was honesty and truth that he sought, even if he sought them in the oddest and, to us, the most perverted places. Baudelaire had the courage to explore the very depths of darkness, (as if he knew that God might also be found there). He shunned nothing, but his tragedy as a man and a poet is that no one can plumb such depths and not either go mad, or else be tainted and corrupted by what he finds. Perhaps the child can do so, but certainly no one else. Baudelaire had the intelligence and sensibility to see what had happened to him, and he said:

> Whether it be during one of those interminable winter evenings, huddled over the fire, or during the hours of summer's dog-days, lost in the corner of some framing-shop, the sight of those drawings never fails to purge me into a deep abyss of contemplation, just as an obscene book always hurls us into the mystic ocean of depression. While gazing at these countless scraps of emotion, samples of Everyman's desires, I have often found myself wishing for some sort of Museum of Love where poets, philosophers, and all interested parties could wander at will, and where everything would have its place, from the almost obsolete devotion of a Saint Teresa to the pedantic excesses of the Eras of Boredom.

It may be thought very strange that I have chosen to consider Baudelaire as an important *Christian* poet. I have done so mainly because I want to demonstrate that to write Christian verse (even that of a hundred years or so ago) was, in the minds of the great writers, an appallingly painful task. So much swept in between them and their work—the materialistic world, the lack of a truly religious tradition and, most of all, the temptations and conflicts which were acted out within the poet's own soul. What, as a novelist, Graham Greene is doing today, Charles Baudelaire felt forced to do a hundred years ago—namely, to explore the depths of Hell, because God might be found there. This, I think, is bravery, not blasphemy. It is easier to love than to believe, but Baudelaire risked the harder choice in his agonizing search for the God who is Truth.

Most critics and other poets, both French and English, have written of Baudelaire. What is probably unique in him is his use of a semi-classical style with a subject-matter that was at the time entirely new. But Baudelaire did not make use of such themes in order to shock anyone; they were simply part of his own individual view of the world, a view which was by no means so bizarre or even blasphemous as some readers have thought. Thus, Mauriac says of him:

> To that Catholic attitude, and that religious dandyism, there corresponds in Baudelaire a heart truly pursued by Grace. A few experiences with opium and hashish, a few excesses with alcohol, do not alter the fact that "the frightening grip of God" weighed on that soul. Whenever I read his poems, I have the feeling that they do not bear their true title. With those three great words, *Flowers of Evil*, at the very threshold of his book, that great poet slanders himself.

How true this is! How little in common there is between the puerile and perverse experiments of our own poetic

traffickers with the devil in the 1890's and this poet, who
was willing to pay the price of great spiritual suffering in
order to meet God—even in Hell itself, if necessary. Saints
have done this, and Baudelaire was, perhaps, not a saint,
though he certainly had the courage to experience himself
all the terrible results of the Fall of Man.

As a Frenchman, Baudelaire was not confronted with
the sort of problems which faced the Catholic nineteenth-
century poet in England. He lived in a world that was
still Catholic, even if that Catholicism often manifested
itself in cheap and sentimental ways. Complacency, too,
was rife among the middle classes, although these classes
still clung to the practice of their religion.

There is, in Baudelaire, not so much a wish to shock
as to lay bare the beauty and terror at the heart of Christianity. As Mauriac points out, "the last of the *Fleurs du
Mal*, 'The Voyage', in a manner unequalled in its splen-
dour, expresses that need of the human heart to escape
from the finite".

After the heart-rending verse of Baudelaire, Péguy, who
might be called the French poet of the 1914 war, seems
calm, almost contented. In fact, he also had his own
problems, since, on account of a marital relationship un-
recognized by the Church, he was unable to receive the
sacraments. Despite this, however, there is a limpid innocence about his work which makes it hard for the reader
to believe that the poet suffered as much conflict as did
Baudelaire.

Péguy is a poet of praise; in some ways, he reminds one
of Traherne. Both are intensely childlike; neither ever
seems to have lost the sense of wonder. Péguy was im-
mensely prolific. Reading him, one feels that he could
never satisfy himself that he had paid sufficient tribute

either to God or the world. In *The Holy Innocents*, he writes:

> O Night shall it be said I created you last,
> And that my Paradise and that my Beatitude
> Will be nothing but a great night of clarity,
> A great eternal night. . . .
>
> In every family, God says, there is a last-born,
> And he is the most cherished.
> My little hope who would dance with a skipping-rope
>   in processions,
> She is in the house of the virtues
> As Benjamin was in the house of Jacob.

The most notable aspect of Péguy's work is what I can only call both the fullness and simplicity of it; it is child-like in the best sense, yet its view of life in this world is profound without ever being complex. In a sense, Péguy is telling us, in all his poetry, the story of God's dealings with man throughout the centuries:

> I have carved time out of eternity, God says,
> Time and the world of time.

Much of the effectiveness of Péguy's work is due to his skilful use of repetition, his extremely straightforward vocabulary, and his long, melodious line. He is not one of the greatest French poets, but he is certainly one of the most underrated. On the whole, the French reader has a marked taste for the gnomic and the lyric; he is not generally addicted to the prolix, or even to the spirit which informs much of Péguy's work. A poet of the 1914 war, and a deeply religious poet at that, it is rather remarkable that his work has endured, and is enduring, for so long.

Paul Claudel, the great modern French dramatist and poet, is an altogether more complex writer than Péguy. A

convert, who entered the Church while at Christmas High
Mass in Notre-Dame, his work continues to be acted, but
I am inclined to think that the prose poems, which often
move towards a condition of prayer, are his finest and
most lasting achievements. Of him, Conor Cruise O'Brien
has written: "in Claudel, the poet and the Catholic are
indissolubly conjoined. He is as completely integrated a
Catholic person as it is given to fallen man to be. The
sincerity of his poetry may be known because of the dark
depths from which it reverberates: *it is not Christian in any
safe or antiseptic way* (italics mine), but is often danger-
ously equivocal."

This is what being a "Catholic" poet really entails—
that is to say, being willing to go to the edge of Hell itself
in search of God and of Truth. The adjective has nothing
at all to do with merely transcribing dogmas or versifying
God's mercy to men. To Claudel, as O'Brien points out,
"the Muse . . . is grace—communication with God through
poetry". When we come to a brief examination of the relations between mysticism and poetry, we shall, I hope, see
precisely what this means.

In Claudel we find the same kind of spiritual struggle
which Baudelaire manifests. The chief difference between
the two men is that where Claudel, in spite of all his
questionings and difficulties, remained a steadfast Catholic
(witness his horror at some of the views and writings of
André Gide), Baudelaire risked the very depths of Hell
itself, not simply as a kind of childish dabbling with evil
but as a full exploration of the dark heart of man. He is a
terrifying poet because he only leaves one tiny chink
through which the ray of hope may shine. In Claudel, however, we are offered much more; as O'Brien declares:

It is power, not grace or sympathy, which affects one in
Claudel: the word as a raw and dangerous force, without

suavity or indulgence. Neither of the two poles of the current of power should be forgotten, for it is not more futile to overlook the predominance in the poet's work of the idea of God than to fail to see that the other pole lies, as Yeats knew:

In the foul rag-and-bone shop of the heart.

George Steiner, the fine young critic, has said interesting things about Claudel in *The Death of Tragedy*. Among English critics, Claudel is a poet and dramatist who has, I think, been unfairly neglected; there seems to be something in his work that is particularly antipathetic to English readers. He is not one of those men who appeal (as Mauriac and Bernanos appeal) to those who are not at one with, or even sympathetic towards, his adamant Roman Catholic beliefs. Steiner is an exception to this, as he shows when he declares:

> Being a dramatist with a bias toward the tragic and also a devout Catholic committed to a view of the world's reality in Christ, Claudel had to meet head on the paradox of Christian tragedy. He resolved it in a manner both trenchant and naïve, as was his nature. Claudel's characters experience destinies which are tragic because they are detours or deflections from . . . God's purpose.

As the centuries proceed, it seems that Catholic poets are confronted with more and more difficulties. I am inclined to think, in fact, that the greater, the finer the poet, the greater the conflict.

Finally, we come to Dante, the greatest of all Christian poets, the flower of the Catholic Renaissance, the man who, perhaps, influenced Chaucer more than any other poet. It is impossible to deal at all adequately with the three parts of his great work, *The Divine Comedy*. At best, one can outline its content and treatment, and indicate where the medieval aspects of Christianity mingle with the

Renaissance, and move towards the modern. Dante's learning must have been fabulous, but he subdued his theological knowledge to the needs of his poem. To us today, of course, it requires a good deal of annotation; it deals with a physical world and a spiritual after-life that have little meaning for most readers. This means, then, that all depends on Dante's fantastic imagination; where people once accepted dogmas implicitly, he must give them at least some plausibility. Just as we enter willingly into the world of *Paradise Lost*, so we must show "that willing suspension of disbelief" when we participate in the strange world of *The Divine Comedy*.

This remains true even for the Catholic and Christian; our ideas of Heaven and Hell have, after all, greatly changed since the medieval ages. What was literal and concrete to Dante is often analogical and spiritual to us. But at least we accept the major dogmas put forth by him. It is, I think, a great tribute to Dante that the agnostic, and even the atheist, can accept, at least temporarily, so strange a world.

The thirteenth century in Italy saw the flowering of all the arts, but Dante was undoubtedly the greatest poet of the period; he influenced our own Chaucer, though, with the exception of *Troilus*, the latter became an almost completely comic, even ribald poet.

Most readers know that Dante's work is traditionally said to have been inspired by one deep glance at Beatrice, a woman he loved and never saw again. There is nothing really bizarre about this; poetry has sprung from stranger sources before, and even from less convincing ones.

Dante was fortunate, too, in living in a world and an atmosphere that contained, accepted and honoured many poets. What is remarkable, however, is the skill and energy which enabled him to write his great epic in *terza rima*, a very difficult form to sustain. A similar remark has been made about *Paradise Lost*, but at least Milton was not working with a language that possesses an almost infinite number of rhymes (and, anyway, the iambic pentameter does not employ rhyme), whereas Dante had at his disposal an inflected language which could not help but limit him with the subtlety of his rhyme-endings; in one sense, therefore, his medium made things very simple for him; in another, it made them almost *too* easy.

The *Paradiso*, or third and final part of the *Comedy*, is almost ineffable; one can only read it and marvel. It is tempting, however, to suppose that Dante took more pleasure in writing the *Purgatorio* and *Inferno*; perhaps all human beings, including great poets, are better at depicting the horrific than the happy. We do, after all, know much more about evil than about good, and there is something in our fallen natures that positively relishes depicting the vicious and the sadistic.

From Dante's great work, it is not so far a cry to a short commentary on the relations between poetry and mysticism. I am here speaking exclusively of Christian mysticism. For some time, it has seemed to me that there is a real relationship between, for example, the overflow of ecstasy which we find in Traherne or Vaughan and their need to express this ecstasy in language. Traherne's lines, "You never enjoy the world aright . . .", and so on, seem more than simply the aftermath of a unique experience of union with God; so, too, do Teresa of Avila's *Autobiography*, the verse and prose of John of the Cross, the poems of Herbert and Crashaw (at his best), Eliot's *Four Quartets*, to give but a few examples.

In works such as these, one feels that the mystical experience itself is only completed by being put into words; to put the matter differently, language is a necessary part of the experience. All this sounds rather heterodox, since the essence of mysticism has usually been regarded as its wordlessness. It is true, I think, that the first vivid vision is bound to fade a little when words intervene. On the other hand, how can a man or woman know what they have experienced until they try to speak about it? Poetry would certainly seem to be the most suitable medium for such explanations.

Much has been dealt with in this chapter, and much has perforce been telescoped. If, however, some faint idea both of the nature of foreign Christian poetry, and also of the place of mystical experience in verse, has been conveyed, then one can only hope that the reader will explore these subjects further for himself. This study, at best, is after all intended only to be "hints and guesses".

CHAPTER X

CONCLUSION

In this chapter I intend to consider mainly the particular problems of the Christian poet today, and also to consider what writers and critics such as Martin Turnell, Auden, David Jones, and others, have said about them. I have no wish to separate Christian verse from any other kind, but it must surely be clear to the experienced reader of poetry that today the Christian not only faces problems which all poets have always faced, but is also confronted with difficulties by the very fact of being a Christian in a materialistic, technological age.

It might have been supposed that a higher class of living, the profusion of paperbacks, and the increasing amount of leisure would have given people more time and opportunity to study and enjoy the arts. With certain exceptions, such as the Third Programme in England, the success of the Penguin Modern Poets series, and the production of much verse on discs, this does not seem to have been so— at least not on any noticeable scale. It is a Communist state like Russia which has done most for its poets and, to judge from the work of the young Yevtushenko (who is an immense success without, apparently, having "to talk down" to his audiences), no "prostitution of one's art" or any of that kind of nonsense has been necessary. On the other hand, the U.S.A. treats its poets quite differently; it provides them with prizes, scholarships and university creative writing jobs, but it cannot, of course, guarantee them an audience. Hence the Beat poets and the other rebels. All these problems are also part of the life of all English poets. Shall the poet have a literary job? Shall he become a freelance writer? Or shall he be a "lay-about" who depends on other people's charity to provide him with a living?

Now, the Christian poet must also reconcile such sociological difficulties as these with his faith and the practice of it. If his beliefs are profoundly felt, then there would seem to be no problem about how he should write and what he should write about; unhappily this is not so. All poets are very delicately attuned to the spirit of their own age; it is very nearly impossible to write alertly and convincingly on a subject in which few others are interested; a poet always writes for an audience—not consciously but very much with one in the depths of his mind. Interplay between poet and reader is essential. It may sound heterodox, but I am fairly sure that a Christian poet must neither conceal his creed, on the one hand, nor preach fiercely about it, on the other. I think he must, and surely will if he has any sensibility at all, move with the technical experiments and (up to a point) the ideas of his age, yet somehow create for his verse a Christian context and background.

As Martin Turnell sees it, the problem for the Christian artist is specifically this:

> There are, broadly speaking, two possible approaches open to him. He may adopt a radically Christian standpoint, disregard (in so far as he can) the changes which have taken place during the past four hundred years, and write resolutely against the grain of his age. Alternatively, he can accept the situation in which he finds himself, and try to give a Christian interpretation of the modern world.

And at the beginning of his book, *Modern Literature and Christian Faith*, he states:

> The problem of literature and belief is a complex one.... We only get a truly Christian work of literature when the writer's whole outlook is informed by his beliefs.

It may seem that I am making altogether too much of this problem. It is certainly true that this is an age of problem-hunting; there are, in fact, far more critical works and books with titles such as *The Need for Clarity*, or *The Dilemma of the Artist*, published today than original works of art. We have become obsessed by "problems" when perhaps we should do better to struggle with the ideas, material and, above all, imaginations which we have been given.

All this is true, but it is not so easy thus to shelve the difficulties of the poet who is a Christian today. A few writers—David Gascoyne and David Jones—seem to exist above and beyond such problems. They create worlds—Blake and Chagall did in paint—which are autonomous; these worlds are not fantasy, far from it, but they are certainly highly personal and would never, in any century, have commanded a wide audience. It does seem rather paradoxical then, that it is David Jones who, in *Epoch and Artist*, has made more profound and valuable remarks about Christian art today than any other writer I know of. He goes far beyond mere "problems" that exist in time and which change from century to century. He is concerned with what is lasting in art and with what is eternal in man. Thus, he declares:

> It is the intransitivity and gratuitousness in man's art that is the sign of man's uniqueness; not merely that he makes things, nor yet that those things have beauty.... With regard to the gratuitous quality which is said to adhere to Art it is well to remember that theologians say that the creation of

the world was not a necessary, but a gratuitous act; . . . and when a painter, referring to a work, uses some such expression as, "That's real fun", we all know that he is not referring to anything funny. *On the contrary, he is referring to a felicitous quality in the painting* [italics mine].

For Jones, art is a sign, a bodying forth of praise or truth or love; for him, God is present in all works of art because man is a *maker*, whether a craftsman or a great artist. By the act of making, he shares in the Divine Act of Creation. Thus, for Jones then, the fashioning of *all* art is a religious act in itself, no matter what its subject-matter may be.

Valéry too, that most abstract of writers, confirms this view, though in very different words. He asserts that "the past has indeed a kind of spiritual energy of a special nature: it is manifested in him and reveals him to himself in certain moments of infinite worth. . . . Literature, then, interests me *profoundly* only to the extent to which it urges the mind to certain transformations—those in which the stimulating properties of language play the chief part. . . ." And Valéry continues by discussing his own working methods and thus takes us outside the limits of this chapter.

The more one thinks of what men like Valéry, Rilke, Eliot and David Jones have said about the dangers and difficulties of being a Christian and a poet today, the more one begins to see that we are dealing with a deeply philosophical and metaphysical question, not simply a literary one.

Of all modern Christian writers, I suppose Eliot has actually enacted in his work this whole philosophical matter. Moving from a distaste for the modern world, manifested in the early poems, to an overtly religious viewpoint in *Ash Wednesday* and *Murder in the Cathedral*, he made his great mystical *Four Quartets* an examination and re-enactment of what this chapter is trying to clarify and simplify. In the last resort, and in the final quartet, *Little Gidding*, Eliot brings together the Incarnation, the material world and man's spiritual life. Disgust is abandoned because he realizes that nothing which God has created can really be disgusting; it is only man's attitude towards it which can make it seem so.

In a very true sense, then, the *Four Quartets* are a great and sensuous poem as well as a philosophical exegesis:

> Gentile or Jew
> O you Who turn the wheel and look to windward
> Remember Phlebas who was once
> handsome and tall as you—

A passage like this is completely at home with fragments such as the following:

> Time before and time after
> In a dim light
>
> . . . . . .
>
> Neither plenitude nor vacancy. . . .

> Over the gloomy hills of London,
> Hampstead and Clerkenwell,
> Campden and Putney,
> Highgate, Primrose, and Ludgate—
> Not here the darkness in this twittering world.

Auden has been very specific indeed in his views of a Christian art, and perhaps this is not so surprising when one remembers the strange material he introduced into his own *Hours* poems. Of the Christian as poet, then, he declares forthrightly and unequivocally that, "The Incarnation, the coming of Christ in the form of a servant who cannot be recognized by the eye of flesh and blood but only by the eye of faith, puts an end to all claims of the imagination to be the faculty . . . which manifests what is truly sacred and what is profane. . . ." Auden thus shares with David Jones the conception of art as a sacred thing; but where the two men differ entirely is in their conception of man as a creator and shower-forth of signs. David Jones would never (and I am sure he is right) maintain that Christ's coming had diminished the mystery in which we all live, and of which the poet is particularly the spokesman, since, if he is not the interpreter of sacred signs, he is assuredly the illustrator, the one who demonstrates them and bodies them forth. In a very different way, Blake would have felt the same thing.

Auden continues: "To a Christian, the godlike man is not the hero who does extraordinary deeds, but the holy man, the saint, who does good deeds." This whole idea seems to me extremely shallow; and Auden, an otherwise profound and original thinker, would seem for once to be oversimplifying an extraordinarily complex subject.

It would appear to me that whatever a poet's beliefs are today, even if they run against the stream of current taste and opinion, they can be *made* acceptable by the skill and integrity of the poet himself. In other media, one can recall the unexpected popularity of Professor Tolkien's prose trilogy, *The Lord of the Rings*. True, this work is a marvellous flight of fantasy and imagination. All the easier, then, it might have been supposed, for Christianity, which is based in history, to be acceptable even to the most sceptical readers. Oddly, this is not so.

I think, perhaps, that what non-Christian readers and writers really object to (and rightly) is Christian verse which either has "a palpable design upon" them, or which, has not outgrown the feeble hymn-like quatrains of the nineteenth century. The Christian writer is in a minority; he must, as it were, do everything for himself, always with the comfortless possibility that no one will want to read him anyway. But at least his work is more profitable than the countless little personal poems which we are always encountering today in volumes of new verse and in some anthologies. If Christianity is a dead tradition, certainly no new one of resonance or value has been found to replace it.

It is, I believe, of extreme interest that Stephen Spender, in a recent number (November, 1964) of *The London Magazine*, makes the following comments: "I suspect too that the whole business about belief has been over-dramatized. There is not the very sharp distinction between what people believed in the past and what they believe now that is supposed. *Probably in the past people thought themselves to believe more than they really did, whereas today we are less unbelieving than we think ourselves to be*" (italics mine).

Perhaps, indeed, each century is more like its predecessor than the dwellers in those epochs want or are prepared to admit. Perhaps all the differences we think we see are mere superficial fashions and not something deep in the hearts and minds of men. I am not entirely sure of this, otherwise, of course, I should not have spent so much time examining this whole question.

What is vital, I think, is that we should all become less self-conscious about our own beliefs and those of the age in which we happen to live. In fact, I would almost go so far as to say that if a great poet writing in Chaucer's style were suddenly to appear on the literary scene, then he would have a right to be taken completely seriously. The trouble is, of course, that such things just do not happen. We are bound to time and to the changes of time; nothing stands still. I have heard (and in part I agree) that what is tedious in Chinese art is the way in which the art of one dynasty so closely resembles that of one hundreds of years later. Novelty in itself has no virtue, but man was surely not intended to create a little eternity of his own in this world. And changes of styles, it must always be remembered, are something more deeply-rooted than mere whims or fashions.

What is lasting in a work of art, whether it be the Parthenon or the ceiling of the Sistine Chapel—and this must be blatantly obvious—is what man finds and has always found means most to him. With shining symbols he celebrates and praises such things as love, innocence, beauty (we enter on difficult and endless ground here, ground which is beyond the scope of this study), and truth. Styles change and dogmas change, but man's needs and desires do not alter. Perhaps one can declare, with a proper humility, that what food is to man's appetite, art is to his spirit.

Here, of course, many will argue that religion satisfies man's spirit, not any of the manifestations of art; my answer to this would be that, at its greatest heights, the two converge. Shakespeare and Sophocles, Keats and D. H. Lawrence, Wordsworth and Eliot, Rembrandt and Rouault —to name but a few—do not differ so very greatly. Eliot himself has named "maturity" as the supreme quality of classical art. Personally, I think that the same quality—to a greater or lesser extent—is to be found in any fine art.

We are dealing with a topic that is endless, and I only have room here to survey one more aspect of it—namely, the detailed symbols and objects which are so often barriers to understanding and pleasure. I do not mean style only (such things as metre, rhyme and rhythm), but rather, say, a chalice in a materialistic age; or satirical humour in a period of serious speculation. Art always has its own battle with time, and not only Christian art.

Finally, if dogma is what makes a poem or a statue a genuine work of art, then there is something fundamentally wrong with art. To this bold remark, many will reply that I am advocating "art for art's sake"; on the contrary, what I want is art for man's sake and for God's sake. And this, at its greatest, is what it is. Petty arguments fall away and we are left with what is Christian because it is true. It may not *seem* Christian, but Christianity is not confined to styles or fashions. Its appeal is to what is deepest in man's mind and heart, and can appear in the oddest places. The only sad thing is that today one has to stress a truth which should be so obvious. But here again, we have a subject which deserves a book entirely of its own.

As I have hinted already, this is an age of arguing rather than of making. My hope is that this short book will encourage the latter without contributing too verbosely to the former. At least, the short amount of space at my disposal has made too much argument impossible.

SELECT BIBLIOGRAPHY

AUDEN, W. H.: *The Dyer's Hand*, London, Faber & Faber, 1963, and New York, Random House, 1962.

GARDNER, Helen (Editor): *The Metaphysical Poets*, Penguin, 1959.

Sir Gawain, translated by Brian Stone, Penguin, 1959.

JONES, David: *Epoch and Artist*, London, Faber & Faber, 1959, and New York, Chilmark Press, 1964.

LEWIS, C. S.: *The Allegory of Love*, London and New York, Oxford University Press, 1959.

LEWIS, C. S.: *The Discarded Image*, London and New York, Cambridge University Press, 1964.

STEINER, George: *The Death of Tragedy*, London, Faber & Faber, 1961, New York, Alfred Knopf, 1961.

TOLKIEN, J. R. R.: *Beowulf, The Monsters and the Critics*, Sir Israel Gollancz Memorial Lecture, 1936.

TURNELL, Martin: *Modern Literature and Christian Faith*, London, Darton, Longman & Todd, 1961, and Westminster, Md., Newman Press, 1961.

ZAEHNER, R. C.: *Mysticism Sacred and Profane*, London and New York, Oxford University Press, 1957.

The Twentieth Century Encyclopedia of Catholicism

The number of each volume indicates its place in the over-all series and not the order of publication.

Titles are subject to change.